Book   ISBN 978-1-7780641-3-5

EBook ISBN 978-1-7780641-4-2

Audio ISBN 978-1-7780641-5-9

What if it's True?

UNLOCKING THE HEART OF THE BIBLE STORY

BILL SPANGLER

This Book Is Dedicated To

All those who attempt to read the Bible but find it
overwhelming and finally give up because they are unable to
navigate their way through its many books, chapters and details.
These pages are for you.

As I place these pages in your hands I resonate deeply
with the words of my good friend
Thandazani Mhlanga

*"I tremble for fear lest I shall belittle the
great story of God by cheap words."*

CONTENTS

Now, some people think the Bible is a book of rules, telling you what you should and shouldn't do. The Bible certainly does have some rules in it. They show you how life works best. But the Bible isn't mainly about you and what you should be doing. It's about God and what he has done.

SALLY LLOYD-JONES

"There are two ways to read Scripture — the way a lawyer reads a will and the way an heir reads a will."

ALEXANDER WHYTE

THE BEGINNING

This book began in a very spontaneous moment. The idea to write it came to me like a lightning bolt right in the middle of a conversation I was having with a friend. She had heard me say that I liked a certain translation of the Bible because of the "earthy street-language" of the text. I had also mentioned that I liked the kind of expression that was used in that translation because it seemed to make it all "so very readable." She asked me what that version was because, she said, "I've tried to read the Bible, but before very long my eyes glaze over and I don't understand what I'm reading, so I put it down."

I told her that I had been referring to the New Living Translation of the Bible. As the conversation unfolded, I made a commitment right then and there. "I need to write a book that presents the narrative of the Bible in a way that people will remain engaged and find the powerful and beautiful message portrayed there before they get lost in the details and set it down." I envisioned it to be an outline that would help people see the big picture. Sort of a GPS to guide them as they navigate their way through the seemingly endless pages of the Bible.

I shared the idea with a few people who have read at least parts if not the entire Bible. They quickly exclaimed, "Well, I need to read a book like that myself! Sometimes I'm a bit lost and a road map would be great." Their interest only added fuel to the spark the initial conversation had ignited, which quickly flared up into a calling that I have not been able to ignore.

The Bible is an amazing book. It has also been described as mysterious, complicated, deep, beautiful, confusing, irrelevant, mythical, and an anchor for the soul. Some call it "The Greatest Story Ever Told."

Some read the Bible as a daily habit, others refuse to read it at all. Some read it out of fear, others cherish it as a source of peace. Some hold it reverently, as a holy book, where others have never opened one, tend to scoff at it, and candidly want to have nothing to do with it at all. Many people see the Bible through the eyes of their personal perception, based on things they have heard or read about it from others, but have never personally taken the time to investigate it for themselves.

Despite the diverse relationships people have with the Bible, it continues to be the annual best seller. Online statistics say the Bible sells almost 55,000 copies per day, adding up to 1.66 million per month, pushing it to 20 million copies per year. The *Guinness Book of Records* claims that in all time, more than 5 billion copies have been sold! Amazon confirms that the Bible is the ultimate #1 best seller. No one book can claim anything even remotely close to that. All of Shakespeare's 42 books together have collectively sold somewhere between 2-4 billion.

A November 2024 online statistic states that the entire Bible has been translated into 756 languages, while portions of it have been translated into an additional 3,000 languages, making at least some part of the Bible available in 3,756 languages or dialects.

Another interesting fact is that the Bible is believed to be the most stolen book of all times. There is something amusingly ironic about stealing a book that teaches "thou shalt not steal!" What is it about this book that causes such interest and a seemingly insatiable desire to have it?

I invite you into a "Drive-Thru" journey through the Bible with me. I am not a theologian, so I can absolutely assure you that we will not get too complicated. I am fascinated by this Book, and I want to make the Bible simple and hopefully allow it to come alive for all those whose "eyes glaze over" when they read it. We will not pause too long at any one place, but hopefully a big picture perspective will be painted in a way that explains a little of why this book stands out among all books and why it is so revered around the entire globe.

In these few "Drones-Eye" view pages, we will pause briefly to specifically notice the history-making, anchoring events outlined here. The main characters of the Bible will be introduced in chronological order, where we will become acquainted with what role they have played and why the events of their lives are noteworthy. Most importantly, we will spend time exploring the life and mission of Jesus Christ, who is without question the leading character of the Bible, zeroing in on why the whole book revolves around Him.

Upon completion of the Bible narrative itself, we will shift to a brief exploration of a few of the significant themes of the Bible which explain its relevance in today's world. The historical saga of Scripture is simply a vehicle written for a much bigger purpose. We will go behind the scenes and seek out the story behind the story.

Nothing in the Bible ultimately matters unless it sheds light on how to navigate the complexity of life that we experience each day. The depiction of the span and scope of life on planet Earth is still being written. While the Bible opens our eyes to how God has interacted with people and nations in history, we also discover insight on how He relates to each of us personally in our day. The last chapters of the Bible shed light on what we are to expect in the near future. Since it is now our turn on the world stage, the background must not be ignored because it provides the context for the role that is ours to play.

As you read these pages, I encourage you to continually ask yourself, "What If It's True?" If it is not true, then the worst that could happen is that you spend a few hours reading some of my thoughts and perspectives on this topic. If it's true, the information in the Bible will be life altering. It is my hope and prayer that something in these pages will answer some of the nagging questions you may have and bring you to a place of peace and calm in the middle of a world that is anything but peaceful and calm. That is what the Bible does for me and is the reason I am sharing my convictions with you.

AUTHOR'S NOTE

I am the first to admit that this book only covers a small portion of what could be delved into when it comes to reading the Bible. There are countless books written on a variety of topics that arise from within the Bible that can be looked up, researched and studied for deeper understanding.

We could discuss at length why the Bible can be trusted and the many aspects that make a case for its validity. Corroborating information from outside the Bible and archeology are viable areas of study that are not addressed here.

The fact that much of the Bible was written by live witnesses of the events recorded could be discussed in depth.

I have not spoken about the many different translations of the original texts or what the purpose new translations really hold for us.

There is an increasing interest in the prophecies of the Bible, especially as the political, economic and cultural fabric of our world seems to be unraveling at an incredible speed. Many are wondering if the Bible speaks to current events. Yes, it does! But prophecy is not explored to any depth in these pages.

I have books in my library that have been written by theologians, teachers, journalists and former detectives who have taken a variety of spiritual, logical or scientific approaches to determining the validity of the Bible. Their conclusions are fascinating to me and are part of the reason I bear the burden to invite you on this journey.

After reading this book you might like to dig a little deeper into some of those topics on your own.

It is not my goal to prove or even thoroughly explain the Bible in detail. It is my goal to just tell the Bible story for you in a simple way and then explain a little bit about why I believe it is so important. While I have made every attempt to accurately portray the unfolding events recorded here, the text of the Bible itself is the final, authentic account. I encourage you to verify my words with the actual words of the Bible themselves.

At the end of each chapter I will share the places in the Bible where you can go to read the details for yourself. My dream for this book is that it will be an appetizer, inspiring you to explore the Bible itself since there is so much more extensive detail there than could ever be written into these few pages.

I will tell the Biblical stories in my own words. Should you see quotation marks around someone's words, I'm only depicting that they are speaking, but not necessarily using a direct quote out of the Scripture. In cases where I do quote directly, I will share the text reference following the quote.

If there is no designated translation listed when I reference a direct quote, it will be from the New Living Translation. If it is from a different translation, I will designate which version it is from.

As I write, it is my opinion that any reference to God, Jesus, or the Holy Spirit should be capitalized. I believe they are Holy, Divine personalities and deserve to be designated differently from reference to friends, family and everyday personalities. You will notice this in my references to those beings.

However, you will also notice when I quote Scripture, in some versions that I reference the translators do not carry the same line of thinking and refer to these beings in lower case. It is simply a preference of mine as I attempt to be reverent when speaking about a Holy God. When you see the capitalized references in my words and then observe it differently from some versions of Scripture, this explains the reason why.

The glasses we wear make an influential difference in the way we see all aspects of life. A blue, red, or yellow tint on our lenses will automatically change the shade of the details we are viewing.

As you read the pages of this book, you may be influenced by things you have previously heard or concluded about the Bible. That is to be expected.

It is my goal to portray the Biblical record just as it is written. You have options. You can put on glasses of skepticism and doubt, questioning the validity of the whole story.

You might read through the lens of "prove it to me," needing to be convinced that there is something worth paying attention to.

There is even the option of seeing these words through the lens of the conviction that "it's all fantasy and fable, but I'll check it out."

I invite you to put on the lens of curiosity, asking "What is the Bible all about? What will I discover if I am open to seeing what the Bible has to say and draw my conclusions after the fact, rather than before I read, based on what I have been told already?"

Start with, "What's the worst that could happen if I read the Bible?"

May you be informed, possibly even surprised, and hopefully inspired by the universal truths God wants to proclaim to us about Himself.

And, what difference would it make if it's true?

1

NO STONE UNTURNED

I have noticed that depending on who I am talking with, there is often a "love it" or "hate it" relationship with the Bible.

As I listen to people speak about the Bible, I can understand and even be empathetic to their experience. Many who have never read the words for themselves have been influenced by what they have been told the Bible says, and unfortunately, they have not always been accurately informed. Others, through their inquisitive musings and their perspective on the deep issues of life, have concluded that the answers they seek would not, or even could not, be addressed in a book as ancient as the Bible. For that reason, they may not even crack open its pages.

We live in an increasingly complex world. The increased, ever-present challenges we face continue to shock our senses, values, and perception of right and wrong. These issues arise in the personal, social, and political spheres that we all are forced to relate to daily. Because these experiences are so personal, it is easy to get caught up in the details, making it difficult to step back and take a careful look at the expanded picture the Bible offers.

I have always had a positive relationship with the Bible. When I was a boy, my family had a set of ten volumes called *The Bible Story*. It was designed for families and every page of each volume had full-color pictures. My mother would read these books to us, and when we finished volume ten, she would start over again at the beginning of volume one. When I was old enough to be able to read, I dug in and read the entire series for myself. Through these books I developed a picture of the Bible and what it was about.

At the other end of the spectrum, there are those who have never been exposed to the Bible. For some it was forbidden, even purposely ignored in their family. For others it was just never made a priority or even considered to be a valuable part of life. I'm grateful that at a very early age I was given the opportunity to read about the fascinating adventures of the Bible characters, and also to come face to face with the wisdom and insights the Bible had to offer.

When the time came to choose a career path, I considered options but was eventually drawn to the study of religion. I received a bachelor's degree in theology and a Master of Divinity degree from Seminary. I have spent many hours reading the Bible, reading about the Bible, and studying commentaries to dig deeper into the meaning of the words and themes presented. I have enjoyed books and articles about themes in the Bible and have been inspired by writings that are both scholarly as well as inspirational and meditative in nature. I have preached from the Bible, and I have spent my life helping others read and learn from the Bible. Of all the things I did as a pastor, my greatest enjoyment came when I had the opportunity to explain the Bible, along with the insight and perspectives that it taught, to people who knew nothing or very little about it.

I passionately believe the Bible provides logical, believable answers to the deep life questions that we ask and that matter to us. I'm convinced that the complex uncertainties we all experience in life are explored and addressed in its pages. In fact, to me the Bible is not just a recommended book, but I hold the conviction that the Bible MUST be read, because of the way it answers the seemingly unanswerable questions of life that may at times keep us awake at night.

Along with all the good and happy experiences we enjoy, at some point every human will encounter events that bring shock, fear, confusion, or pain. It might be from the news we hear daily, or something closer to home such as some despicable act from the hand of a stranger, friend, or even a loved one. The wound may even be self-inflicted, or it may be that we are forced to experience betrayal. Often life seems to be totally unfair or unjust, and the ability to cope seems out of reach. We seek out counselors and wise people whom we trust, and they can be very helpful. However, the wisdom and insight the Bible has to offer as a book of answers and comfort remains a resource that is untapped by so many.

Life often fails to materialize into the desires or dreams we had for the way it was all supposed to play out. In contrast, we are told that there is in fact an all-powerful God who can do anything. He is also portrayed as loving and kind. The obvious question that forms in our minds is, "If God is all-powerful, loving and kind, explain why 'this' happens? Why is the whole world such a mess? Why is MY world such a mess?"

It's a significant and relevant question. For far too many, the question comes up with no logical answer, so they conclude that the idea of a powerful, loving God must in fact be a myth. Naturally one conclusion would be, "why bother to read a book that suggests otherwise?"

In fact, the Bible tackles these very issues, in depth. The problem of pain, suffering and evil in the world, and how God deals with it all is the underlying theme of the whole Bible. There are four queries that we all would like to have answers to. Regardless of culture, race, gender, or nationality the search is the same. What aspect of life as you know it does not relate in some way to these four questions?

- **Where did I come from and how did I get here?**

- **Is there a purpose and meaning for my life?**

- **How do we explain the relationship between the good and evil we see in the world?**

- **What happens when I die? Is this all there is?**

The search for these answers makes up the essence of the spiritual journey. It is the pursuit to find satisfactory insight into questions that are on a different plane than the routine decisions we face every day. Issues relating to our souls, immortality, life after death, Heaven and Hell, wisdom, values, and truth. These topics, as well as the knowledge of and the possibility of relationship with supernatural beings, all come into play in the search for spiritual meaning.

The fascination people have with spirituality is demonstrated by the amount of time and money that is spent in the search surrounding these issues. There is no shortage of books, teachers, spiritual leaders, fortune tellers and mystics offering answers for these deep questions. There is a fascination with tarot cards, palm readers, Ouija boards, classes, shamans, healers, sages, and wisdom keepers offering their best guidance. All of these are seen to be genuine alternative possibilities to the myriad of churches, pastors, and television preachers that are available. The desire is to know the unknown, and in this quest, many choose to search out any possible option that may provide enlightened insight and perspective.

The challenge with all of this is that without any particular guard rails or anchor points to guide them, many often conclude that since there are so many options, any answer they find that logically "makes sense" must be good enough and they settle with that as the final answer. Personal logic now becomes their anchor point, and in the end, each person's "makes-sense-to-me" perspective becomes the final authority for the answers to life's spiritual questions. Accessing the words and thoughts of others enables them to articulate the position they already believe or have been searching for all along. It then boils down to: "If it feels right to me, it must be good. You find 'right' for you, run with that, and we will all just get along."

For some, the search is open to read any book, listen to and consider any teacher with a claim of knowledge or insight in spiritual matters, but closed to even consider what the Bible might have to say. The Bible is viewed by many to be irrelevant, untrustworthy, and even inconsequential. It is ultimately rejected as being a possible resource option in the quest for truth and meaning.

We will discover that all four of these questions are addressed in the pages of the Bible. The Bible does not make defense or argument for its answers. It lays out a grand panoramic perspective, and as each new scene comes into focus, these issues are addressed through biographies, stories, parables, history, culture, teaching, theological discourse, poetry, prose, prophecy, and declaration. And through it all, as we read this grand story, we are able to find clarity as we begin to gain insight into the big picture of God and His role in our world.

If we knew there was treasure under some unknown rock in the field by our house, would we not turn over every single one until we found it? Would we ever say, "I'm not going to bother with that rock. It doesn't look very appealing and probably won't be hiding the treasure I'm looking for anyway?" Nope! I'm sure we would leave no stone unturned.

Not one of the books in my library claim anything remotely close to what the Bible claims. Would it not demonstrate wisdom to at least be open to look into something that makes such bold assertions? If nothing else, what's the worst that could happen if one took the time to read the Bible, even once? People read novels, literature, documents and summaries of information all the time, not because they agree with them, but because they want to explore ideas and insight from others. There is always valuable information out there waiting to be discovered.

What if the Bible is the very resource you have been looking for all along to find direction or peace around those soul-searching questions? What if this is actually the very rock that you have been looking for? What if it's true?

Abraham Lincoln enjoyed asking a fun and curious question. With a twinkle in his eye he would inquire, "If you call a dog's tail a leg, how many legs does it have?"

No matter the length of discussion, his final answer would always be, "The dog has four legs. Calling a tail a leg does not make it a leg."

It is like that with Biblical declarations. Reading a declarative statement and simply writing it off by saying, "Well, I don't agree with that!" changes nothing.

To agree or disagree with something I might read in the Scripture does not change anything about whether it may or may not be true. A statement is not correct because I agree with it, nor is it incorrect if I don't. My acceptance or disagreement of any item or topic does not in any way alter its impact on my life. Truth is always truth. Facts are always facts.

2

THE BIBLE DECLARES

There are typically only six types of speech within the language that we use. Whenever we speak, our words are always made up of some aspect of these six: a request, an offer, a promise, an assessment, an assertion, or a declaration.

When we are making a request, we are asking someone for something either for ourselves or on behalf of another. We may ask for something such as a favor, a loan, a gift, or an act of service of some type.

On the flip side of a request, we could be making an offer, such as when we suggest that there is something we would like to do, or be willing to do, for another person or group of people.

A promise is a commitment we are verbally expressing. More than an expression of an idea, it is a verbal guarantee of our intention to fulfill the action we are expressing.

Then there is an assessment, where we make an appraisal, or an evaluation of an item, a person, an idea, or a statement. It could be an opinion or even a judgment, but ultimately, it's an assessment.

Assertion is a close relative to assessment. To assert something is to take a position that one is willing to back up with facts or evidence. More than a suggestion or a hypothesis, it is a statement that one is prepared to defend.

And lastly, a declaration is a statement that is an explicit, formal proclamation. It is more than an assertion and is different from any of the others already listed. There is no need or intention of defending or providing evidence for a declaration. The one wearing the royal crown would send a messenger out in front of the procession with a declaration that the monarch was about to appear. The messenger would declare, "Hear ye, hear ye! I present to you the king/queen!" There is no need to defend a declaration. They are stated without hesitation or question.

A declaration can only be made by one who has the entitled authority to make the declaration. When the President of the International Olympic Committee is ready, he steps up to the microphone at the beginning of the Olympic games, making a declaration that the games are "now open." At the closing ceremonies, he makes another declaration that the Olympic games are "now closed." And when he says they are open, the games are indeed open, and they begin. When he says they are closed, the games end and the Olympic Games are over. Everyone then goes home. It is not true simply because of the fact or words of the declaration, but also because of the authority of the one who is making the declaration. Those are not hard words to memorize or repeat, but if Bill Spangler got up to the microphone and said the exact same words, the statement would be meaningless because I would not have the right or authority to make such a declaration.

Electricity declares that it will shock us if we touch the wrong wires. And it does! Every single time. Gravity declares that it will always pull us or items toward the center of the earth. Always! With no exception. No one argues with electricity or gravity. We never say, "Well, it can't be accurate 100% of the time. I'm going to just jump out of an airplane without a parachute and simply will myself to float gently to the ground below." Some things just are, regardless of our acknowledgement or disagreement with them.

The Bible continually makes declarative statements; far too many for me to document here. One of the reasons the Bible is a book that cannot be simply ignored, is because of the numerous declarative statements it contains. Declarations are either true or they are not. Some declarations really have no consequence on our personal lives. However, it would demonstrate wisdom to pause and seriously reflect upon any declarative statement that may have personal implication, consequence, or impact.

The Bible is written by humans who believed they had been given a message from God to share with others, even the whole world. They would prayerfully write these messages out in their own words, or verbally speak them to a local gathering. God did not sit and have the writers take a word-for-word dictation although sometimes God does directly speak and is specifically quoted.

The Bible claims to be a record of the wishes of God for mankind, the teachings of God, and the interactions of God in history and in the lives of specific individuals or nations. If God is the one making the declarations we find in the Bible, would it not be wise to at least take note of them?

I will share a few examples.

The Bible declares: "In the beginning, God created the heavens and the earth." Genesis 1:1. That's it, a simple declaration. It does not go on to defend that statement or in any way try to prove it.

In this verse we are informed how life began. We are here because God intentionally created the heavens and the earth. It also declares that the first persons of the human race were created during creation week. The Bible does not argue or discuss it with us. The simple sentence informs us that there is a God, and that He is the creator of life. It is in direct opposition to the idea that life spontaneously started countless centuries ago and through time progressed to what we are today. This declaration means there is a God who is able to create and design life on purpose. There is dignity and purpose for our lives in this sentence.

The Bible declares: "For I am convinced that nothing can separate us from God's love. Neither death nor life, neither angels nor demons, neither our fears for today nor our worries about tomorrow—not even the powers of hell can separate us from God's love. No power in the sky above or in the earth below—indeed nothing in all creation will ever be able to separate us from the love of God that is revealed in Jesus Christ our Lord. Romans 8:38,39.

Here is a declaration that no matter what we may have heard about God being distant and removed from us, or being a harsh dictator, it is simply not true. Many people believe that God is a tyrant. They believe He is watching in order to catch us sinning and then takes pleasure in condemning us. The belief of this lie is one of the reasons people decide they do not ever want to read the Bible. And who can blame them? Who would want to read about a God like that?

We are emphatically informed here that there is nothing that can separate us from His love which is displayed in the life of His Son, Jesus Christ. This means that no matter what we have done, we are not automatically separated from His love. He is out to win our hearts, not condemn or destroy us. The numerous lies about God's anger, condemnation and judgment are exposed by the simplicity of this one statement, let alone many, many others.

The Bible declares: "For God so loved the world, that he gave his only begotten Son, that whoever believes in him should not perish, but have eternal life." John 3:16 (NASB)

The previous declaration states that God always loves. This one, made by Jesus Himself, goes beyond words, and declares that God demonstrated His love by giving us the only Son He had. Here we also learn that the difference between having eternal life or perishing depends upon whether or not we believe in this Son, Jesus.

The urgent reality of this declaration is that there are eternal consequences attached to it. The statement declares that there are two options ahead of us. We either perish, (die forever) if we don't believe in this Son, or we receive eternal life if we do believe in this Son. It is literally a life and death matter.

The Bible declares: "When everything is ready, I will come and get you, so that you will always be with me where I am." John 14:3.

These are the words of Jesus, Himself, His own direct promise. Long before Douglas MacArthur said, "I will return," and Arnold Schwarzenegger said, "I'll be back," Jesus promised His friends and all of us, "I will come and get you." Do we trust Him? The overarching theme of the Bible is God's work on our behalf to restore the relationship which He originally had in mind when He created us. His words are in fact a guarantee. This is the final event the world is heading for.

The Bible declares: "For He has set a day for judgment with justice." Acts 17:31

I don't include this statement to startle or cause fear. I include it to say that the Biblical worldview includes an ending to life as we know it on planet Earth. There is an indescribable intention for what happens next. The world we live in now is not going to just carry on indefinitely or end in some global catastrophe. God has a plan, a victorious, restorative plan.

While justice in our court systems is often tainted by human perspective, we are assured here that this judgment will be different, meaning it will be fair and will be done with transparent integrity. We may have good reasons for suspicions about the fairness and justice of human judges, but this judgment will be done by God Himself. There is nothing to fear if the outcome will be the justice meted out by a Holy God, whose signature attributes and motivations are love and mercy.

I share these five statements out of hundreds of declarations that the Bible makes to offer a sample of how life-altering the message of the Bible truly is. What difference does it make in my life if they are in fact true?

The point I am wanting to present is nicely illustrated by the anecdote of the ship captain who was out on the dark waters guiding his battleship forward through the night. Ahead he saw a blinking light that seemed to be on a direct collision course with his battleship. He signaled to the ship ahead, asking that it alter its course ten degrees to the North.

Almost immediately the light ahead signaled back that the captain needed to alter his course ten degrees to the South in order to avoid a collision. The captain was not impressed with the arrogance of whoever sent that message. He sternly responded that he was Captain Jones and that he was ordering the oncoming vessel to alter its course ten degrees to the North. The reply informed the captain that this message was coming from Private Smith, and that Captain Jones should turn his ship ten degrees to the South.

The captain became angry at the obvious insubordination of the private and without hesitation fired back that he was the captain of a loaded battleship and was prepared to fire unless the ship ahead turned its course ten degrees to the North. The reply quickly came back that read, "This is a lighthouse. Adjust your course ten degrees to the South." That was the end of the discussion. The humbled captain adjusted his course without further dialog.

I love this illustration as it opens our eyes to the many implications around assumptions, perceived authority, and the "I'm Right" stance we are so prone to take in life. Private Smith had a declaration to make. "This is a Lighthouse." There was no further need for discussion or proof. Captain Jones could alter his course accordingly, or smash onto the rocky seashore. We are reminded how quickly we may need to alter our position when new or different information becomes evident, especially when it demonstrates itself to be correct.

Is it possible that the Bible might be the ultimate lighthouse in the darkness of the world that cries out to us to alter our courses before we destroy ourselves? Could it be a warning from a loving God?

God is like electricity. *We all enjoy the benefits of electricity and would really struggle to live without it. We depend on electricity for light, for heat, for water and to provide hot showers. We experience countless options for entertainment, operating our tools, as well as cooking and baking. We love what it offers.*

On the other hand, electricity is more powerful than we are and must always be respected. If raw energy were to come directly into our houses, they would burn, hot and quick. We cannot work with electricity that is not moving through a transformer to bring it to a power level that makes it usable for us.

God is like that. He wants us to know Him, and He wants to be close to us, but if He were to show up and sit beside us without any type of protection for us, His holiness would instantly overwhelm and consume us in our human condition. However, because He loves us and wants to be in relationship with us, He covers Himself in whatever way necessary so that we can interface with Him. That's how important we are to Him.

In the Bible narrative we are about to read, we will find incidents where sinful human beings defied Him, challenging His divinity. While God's purpose is totally love centered, there are times when He reveals more of Himself and His majesty than humans are comfortable with, or are able to manage. We learn from these incidents that worship, awe and reverence before this God is always the appropriate position to take.

We would never take electricity for granted and start handling bare wires. As created beings whom God loves, we should be always grateful for the power He demonstrates on our behalf but never take it for granted and decide that we can order Him around. God always knows what is best and we are blessed when we bow to His sovereign wisdom.

This is what the LORD says—your Redeemer and Creator: "I am the LORD, who made all things. I alone stretched out the heavens. Who was with me when I made the earth?"

ISAIAH 44:24

O Sovereign LORD! You made the heavens and earth by your strong hand and powerful arm. Nothing is too hard for you.

JEREMIAH 32:17

You are worthy, O Lord our God, to receive glory and honor and power. For you created all things, and they exist because you created what you pleased.

REVELATION 4:11

3

HOW EVERYTHING BEGAN

Enough preliminaries! I am excited to share with you a simple overview of the Bible, from Genesis through to the book of Revelation. The Bible does not record the secular history of all the nations in the world but instead is a record of God's spiritual work of salvation for all people everywhere. God chose to do His work for all mankind through one family, who became a nation of people. Just because the Bible does not record the history of the rest of the nations on the earth does not mean they were not important to God. This record is about how all nations matter to God and what He is doing on their behalf.

I will point out the highlights of the history that is recorded here, along with the major players as they come along, and the location of where these events took place. We will follow along in chronological order. Fasten your seat belts and let's get started.

The Bible begins with the book of Genesis. Even the word Genesis means "beginning" or "origin". The book of beginnings. There are so many firsts in this book.

With no pretense or introduction, the first words simply read that God created the heavens and the earth. Along with the universe, sun, moon and stars, all planets, plants, animals, fish, birds, and human beings were also created. All of it. Nothing found its way here outside of the creative imagination, and the miraculous, omnipotent words of

God. (Omnipotent simply means there is no limit to what God is able to do. Omni-potent. All powerful.)

Imagine! God was able to bring things into existence, with authority, simply by using His voice and creative power. This is way more exciting than being able to smash crystal glasses by hitting the right note on the scale as some have been known to do!

When God said the words, "Let there be trees," forests appeared. The voice of God could produce willows, pine, cedar, poplar, redwood and bamboo trees, along with all the others, each with its own perfect characteristics and unique details.

He created birds, fish, flowers and stars. He divided the land from the water making lakes and rivers. All with His voice!

The words of God brought forth giraffes, puppy dogs, horses and elephants. All creatures large and small, on the same day. Each with a mate for the purpose of procreation.

As so often is the case, the best part came last! On the 6th day of creation, God said, "Let's make someone like Ourselves, in Our image." In other words, someone They could talk to, relate to, converse with, love and receive love from in return.

Who is the "Us" and "They"?

Allow me to take a short detour and insert a word picture here that may help to unravel a mystery. God is so often referred to as "He," singular, but when man was created the words are "Let's" make someone like "ourselves," in "our" image. All plural references.

When we hold an egg in our hand we have a shell, a white, and a yolk. We can separate them into three separate entities. We can use eggshells alone for decoration while egg whites and egg yolks have separate nutritional cooking or baking purposes. We would not hold up an eggshell and say this is an egg. Nor would we say the same for the white or the yolk. But when all pieces are together we simply call it an egg.

The Bible explains to us that God is demonstrated to us through three separate persons. God, the Father, God, the Son, and God, the

Holy Spirit, sometimes referred to as the Holy Ghost. We have three separate entities, the Father, the Son, and the Holy Spirit. All together we simply refer to them as God. Therefore, sometimes the Bible will refer to God in singular form, and sometimes plural language may be used.

What a powerful statement the creation of mankind makes about the dignity and purpose of humanity. God wanted to create beings who could expand the possibilities for relationship and the expression of love. Created in the image of God to reflect His character.

We read with fascination that the first man, Adam, was formed from dust. Then, when each detail was in place and everything was ready, God knelt down and breathed into his nostrils "the breath of life." Instantly his heart began to beat, his lungs began to breathe, his blood began to circulate. He opened his eyes and came alive. Incredible! Imagine taking your first breath as an adult, fully able to get up and walk around and speak with a full vocabulary. And the first person you would talk to and see is God Himself!

This is the Biblical declaration of the beginning of human life and the origin of mankind. Designed with loving dignity by the hand of a Creator God. Nothing random or chance about it.

Adam noticed that all other creatures had a mate. However, there was no one like himself. No one to compliment him, talk to him, or be a companion for him.

God, the master anesthesiologist, caused him to go into a deep sleep, during which He took a rib from Adam's side. Out of that rib he created a partner for Adam. A woman. I can only imagine how stunning they both were. Barbie and Ken would be no comparison to how perfect this couple would have been.

"Handsome" could not begin to fully describe Adam, and "beautiful" would not be a word magnificent enough to embrace all that would portray Eve. They were a perfect match. Together with their complimenting features, they were complete, able to procreate and fill the earth with offspring who would also be born in the image of God.

God instructed them to have children and fill the earth with people like themselves.

They lived in a garden called Eden, which is believed to have been somewhere in the area of what is Northern Iraq today. That Eden paradise was incomparable to anything we know today, no matter how beautiful our favorite places might be.

At the end of each day of creation, God would look upon what had been created and would say, "It is very good." I think that probably meant, "Perfect!"

Sadly, the perfect life in paradise did not last long. We don't know how long, maybe weeks or months or even years, but one day it all came to a crashing halt!

Chapter three of Genesis records the event that brought about the beginning of sin, the day when all that perfection was destroyed by one person, who made one fatal decision.

Adam and Eve were created for the purpose of love and relationship, with God, with each other, and with their offspring.

God told them they could eat and enjoy any fruit from any tree in the entire garden, with one exception. The exception was a tree in the center of the garden that was called the Tree of the Knowledge of Good and Evil. He added that if they ate the fruit from that tree, they would surely die.

That's a simple request, is it not? It wasn't that the fruit was poisonous. The implication was that should they eat from the fruit of the one tree that God had explicitly warned them not to eat from, they would be making the deeper statement that they didn't believe God. It would be a statement of disregard, in fact challenging God, defiantly suggesting that they could get away with doing exactly what God had said they should not do. The action would state that they believed He was not telling them the truth.

The Bible has a backstory that is not told here in Genesis but is spelled out in other places in the Bible. We come to find out that God had an enemy. Almost inconceivably, this enemy at one time had been the angel Lucifer, the leader of all the angels in Heaven. He had become hostile toward God and was cast out of Heaven along with one third of the angels there who sympathised with him. Instead of Lucifer the angel, he became known as Satan, the enemy of God.

Satan had been cast down to planet Earth, and was lurking in the garden, watching for a way to entice either Adam or Eve to question or even disobey God. Since he hated God, he also hated all God's children and would do anything to disrupt their peace, harmony and relationships.

On that fateful day, disguised as a serpent, he appeared in the garden to meet Eve at the very tree that was to be avoided. If she had stayed away from the tree God had said to avoid, the enemy would have never had a place to even engage in dialogue with her. But here she was, much to his delight and he started by questioning her recollection of what God had in fact said to her about this tree. He asked if God had said there were any trees in the garden they could not eat from.

The fact that here was a talking serpent no doubt startled her, (how can you not be intrigued by a talking serpent?) but she engaged in conversation and replied that yes, God had said that they should not eat of the fruit of this very tree in the center of the garden. She added that He had said if they ate fruit from this tree they would actually die.

The enemy used this fact to set his snare and zeroed in on her trust in God. He lied to her and emphatically sneered, "You aren't going to die!", insinuating that God was openly lying to them. Then he teased her imagination by suggesting that God was in fact withholding something very precious. He enticingly added, "Actually, when you eat this fruit, you will gain wisdom and be just like God."

This was a moment in time that carried universal consequences. The test was simple but profound. Where was her loyalty focused? Would she trust God, obey Him and stand unwavering in her belief of His words of caution? Or would she fall for the serpent's philosophical trap and instead place her trust in him and his enticing words?

I've written countless tests and quizzes at various times during my years of education, but good grades in school were not even close to the consequences of passing or failing this test.

Sadly, she took the bait. She chose to believe Satan instead of God, and ate from the tree, expecting to receive the wisdom of God as the enemy had told her she would. Instead, she became wise in the ways of sin, the things that God did not want her to ever have to experience. When she gave some fruit to Adam, he ate it too, and together they faced the consequence of their decision.

Everything changed! Immediately they felt shame and distance from the God who had created and loved them. He visited with them daily and they had never experienced fear of Him before. But this time, on the same day they ate the fruit, they hid when He came to visit. When God called out to them they finally appeared out of the bushes. As they began to talk, Adam blamed Eve for eating the fruit and then bringing some of it to him to eat. He went even further, seeking to blame God for all this when he said, "This woman you gave me." Eve in turn passed the buck and blamed the serpent, because he "deceived me." It was a most tragic day in so many ways.

There was another tree in the garden called the Tree of Life. Eating the fruit of this tree was symbolic of the never-ending, life-giving relationship His created ones would have with God. Their faith in God allowed them access to the Tree of Life and as they continued to enjoy its fruit, they would live forever.

Now that they had displayed faith in the word of the enemy over His word, God sadly knew that Adam and Eve could no longer dwell in the garden because people who did not trust Him should never enjoy access to the Tree of Life and expect to live forever. Without access to this tree, they would die.

God took Adam and Eve out of the garden, and angels stood at the entrance so that they would not ever be able to return to it. Every generation from then until today has been born without access to the Tree of Life. The impact of their disobedience not only affected them, but it also sold out the whole human race. We live in a broken world today because of their decision to disobey God that day. They learned the hard way that disregarding God's wisdom, and trusting someone other than God Himself, always has serious consequences.

They did not suffer these consequences because they ate an apple, or whatever the fruit actually was. Eating the forbidden fruit was an act of distrust that interrupted the life-giving connection that God had with His created beings. Death would overcome them, as well as every one of their descendants, unless some solution could be found.

As Adam and Eve experienced the result of their decision, we probably have no comprehension of the depth of their regret. Their first son murdered his own brother. How gut-wrenching it must have been for them to deal with the body of their lifeless son, knowing that death came to him ultimately as a result of their disobedience.

Their beautiful bodies, straight from the hands of their Creator, began to deteriorate. They had been created to live forever, but although they lived to be over 900 years old, they eventually died, as God had said. Their decision at that tree disrupted everything God had planned and designed for mankind.

Adam and Eve's children would also have children as the offspring began to procreate and fill the earth. This meant that there was no option except for siblings to have children together. There was no other race or family to marry into. While this practice is not advised or even legal today in many countries, we must remember that the strong genetic makeup of the direct descendants of Adam and Eve would not present the same health risks we would experience today. Mixing family genes is not advised today due to thousands of years of weakening health and physical stamina. They lived to be over nine hundred years old, and we get a congratulatory letter from the Prime Minister and the King if we should make it to one hundred!

Tucked into that dialogue on the day they ate the fruit is a promise made to Adam, Eve and the serpent. The declaration was made by God Himself that someday a descendent of theirs would finally defeat and destroy the serpent for what he had done. Also, not only would the enemy be destroyed, death itself would also be defeated. A Savior would come, and through His work all things would be restored and made perfect again.

That very promise is the connecting theme of the Bible from beginning to end. The Bible is a record of the work of God and how far He was willing to go to fulfill that promise. It is God's ultimate and only purpose to return us to the relationship He originally designed for us, where we will live forever without death overshadowing our existence.

For several hundred years, God sadly took note of the decline of mankind's interest in spiritual matters, finally reaching the nearly complete and utter degradation of humanity. We read, "The Lord observed the extent of human wickedness on the earth, and he saw that EVERYTHING they thought or imagined was consistently and totally evil." Genesis 6:5 (Emphasis mine) Just think, every thought or imagination, was consistently and totally evil. How dark life becomes when disconnected from the creator God.

This insidious sinful mindset was about to entrap all living persons on the earth. In order to preserve His goal of restoring His relationship with them, He realized that He must intervene. He decided to send a flood that would demonstrate His ultimate sovereign authority over sin and the work of the enemy. Man must remember that we can push against God only so far. His mercy never ends for those who want to be in relationship with Him, but like electricity, we must remember that His power is not controlled by the choices and desires of sinful mankind.

In spite of His plan, still God's mercy ruled. He offered a way of safety through the flood to anyone who wanted it, should they choose to accept it. God searched for someone who still honored Him and found a man named Noah. God invited him to build a floating boat, an ark, big enough to house everyone who would choose to enter. This ark was also to be big enough to accommodate all the species of animals that He would use to repopulate the Earth on the other side of the flood. An angry, vengeful, condemning God would not have bothered to offer a way of escape. He would have just wiped everything out and cleaned the slate.

For more than one hundred years, Noah worked on building the ark. As he worked, he preached and pleaded with people to plan and be ready to come on board in order to be safe during the flood. The people laughed and scoffed at his foolishness, reminding him that it had never rained at any previous time in the history of planet Earth. Questioning his sanity, they no doubt asked, "Who in their right minds builds a ship on dry land with no place to float it?" When the ark was finished, despite all his pleading and warning, it turned out that Noah, his wife, their three sons along with their sons' wives were the only eight people who walked up the ramp into safety. Everyone else on the planet rejected the invitation.

This is a specific example of God teaching us about His character and how He could both be a God of justice and a God of mercy. He gave a warning as to what was coming, then made provision for and offered safety and freedom to all who wanted to avail themselves of it, but allowed each one to choose for themselves. This picture of God never changes through the entire Bible. As He relates to the sinful condition of the world, He offers grace yet always respects people's choices. He did not force or drag anyone up the ramp into the ark.

Imagine the commotion when one day, without human guidance, animals of all species ambled in from various locations and entered the ark. Some were in groups of two, some in groups of seven. No doubt that scene would cause some people to take a sober second thought, but in the end, it never changed anyone's mind.

Then, without warning, the massive ark door swung closed by the power of unseen hands and was securely sealed. There were only eight persons on board, and there would be no changing of minds. No second chances. People were either in or out of the safety of the ark.

For seven days nothing changed. With bated breath everyone waited, wondering what would happen next. The sun continued to rise and set as it always had. Can you picture the jungle of news broadcasters who would be camped outside the ark if this were to happen today? Each reporting on, well, basically nothing. Everything was normal. There was no rain. Noah's family, and the animals were still waiting inside. One day still followed another, nothing noteworthy. There would not be much new news. It was probably a bit eerie!

No doubt people outside the ark who saw the door mysteriously close must have breathed a bit easier with each passing day. There were likely many events of teasing and hammering on the ark, asking Noah how it was going in there with the animals, scoffingly giving him a weather report of "how nice and sunny it is out here!" Those must have been excruciatingly long days for Noah and his family. "Did we miss something here? Was God really in all of this?"

Then, everything changed on day eight! The sun did not come up at all. It was a cloudy day, and water began to fall from the sky. In torrents! Even fountains from deep in the earth burst open, so there was water falling and water gushing up from the ground. There was no place of safety outside of the ark. As people scrambled to higher ground for safety, they were quickly overcome by the rising water. The deluge lasted for 40 days and nights before the rain finally stopped.

Every living person, bird and creature on the earth that were not in the ark perished. It took five months for the flood waters to recede enough for the ark to settle again. When it did, the great ship was somewhere in the mountain range called Ararat, along the border of today's Turkey and Iran.

Altogether, Noah, his family and the animals were on the ark for over a year. When they emerged, the landscape of the entire world was drastically changed from what it had been when they went into the ark. When the great ark door mysteriously opened again, there were only eight people on the whole planet. What they saw must have been totally devastating. They were alone. Life as they had known it was forever gone. Even the landscape was unrecognizable. It was as if they were living on another planet.

Along with the need to build shelter and places to live, they also had to find ways to grow food again and sustain themselves. They were instructed once again to repopulate the earth, just as God had asked of Adam and Eve. The animals began to spread out over the earth. The little families began to grow, and once again, just like after the Garden of Eden, everyone was related. There was no choice but to marry siblings or first cousins. As the decades went by, the population expanded and life moved on.

God promised them that each time they saw a rainbow, it was a reminder of His commitment to them that He would never again destroy the whole earth with a flood. While cities and communities still experience severe damage and loss from local floods, God's promise that there would be no severe, world-wide event, has held fast. The rainbow is His signature of guarantee.

Human nature was set on a downward trajectory ever since that fateful day in Eden. As the world began to repopulate, the bent of the human heart continued to demonstrate the self-centeredness that exists there. The people after the flood decided that although they had been instructed by God to spread out and populate the earth, they would instead do as they chose. They determined to build a city with a tower that would keep them close and bind them all together. The city and tower, called the tower of Babel, (Bay-bel) were being built somewhere in the region that we would know as Iraq today.

God stepped in and interrupted their plans in a most fascinating and creative way. One day, with no explanation, groups of people began to speak in a variety of different languages. (Does this provide a hint as to why the popular online language learning course is called Babbel?) Construction on the tower completely stopped because they could not understand or communicate with each other anymore. A call for nails, hammers and boards might receive mortar, shovels and water! It was utter chaos and confusion.

In the end, they separated and left with the people they could understand and converse with. Those who spoke one language went together and eventually started making and eating perogies. Another group who could understand each other went in a different direction and found that tacos and burritos were their favorite choice of food. I am thrilled that one group created pizza but am still working on my appreciation for the sushi that yet another group invented. Group after group moved away from each other, and the nations of the earth were born.

You can read full details of all these events in Genesis chapters 1 through 11.

GOD WANTS US TO REMEMBER:

- We have been created and given life by the hand of a designer, not from events triggered by random chance.

- We have been created with purpose. There is always a reason for creating or designing something. Creation by a designer God provides dignity for each life.

- When Adam and Eve believed the serpent and disobeyed God's instruction, their decision sold out their offspring as well as the entire human race that followed. Everyone will die unless there is an intervention.

- That intervention is promised, which is the connecting theme of the entire Bible.

- The roots of good and evil are identified when we see the loving plan of God and the destructive intention of the enemy of God. Right and wrong/good and evil may be easily identified depending on whether the event, action or word results in the love and harmony God desired, or the brokenness and pain motivated by the evil work of the enemy.

- The stories of the flood and the Tower of Babel inform us that God will not let the effects of evil go on unchecked forever. He will guide the course of history as He needs to with boundaries according to His wisdom. He is the ultimate judge of all things and He will respond at the appropriate time. And even in an act of judgment such as the flood, He provides an ark of safety for anyone who wants to take advantage of it. His intention is always for our well-being and our salvation should we choose to take advantage of it. It is a choice left up to us.

The Devil did not tempt Adam and Eve to steal, to lie, to kill, to commit adultery; he tempted them to live independent of God.

BOB JONES, SR.

It wasn't raining when Noah built the ark. Everyone laughed at him until it started to rain. Keep trusting God and keep building!

ANONYMOUS

"Come, let's build a great city for ourselves with a tower that reaches into the sky. This will make us famous and keep us from being scattered all over the world." Genesis 11:4 The people who created the Tower of Babel showed tremendous unity, but they were united against the will of God. It is better to be divided by truth than united in error.

ANONYMOUS

4

GOD CHOSE A FRIEND

The events of the first eleven chapters of Genesis covers a period of approximately two thousand years. There is not a lot of detail. Each event the Bible recorded that had taken place on the earth thus far had involved every person on the planet. These four events provide the backdrop for the rest of the Bible. An introduction of sorts.

Creation was perfect. The enemy infiltrated the perfect setting and got Eve and then Adam to believe a lie about God. They accepted the serpent's lies to them that they in fact would not die if they ate the fruit and instead would become wise like God. Immediately their love turned from Him and focused on their inward fear and insecurities. Their son murdered his brother. The world became so dark and evil that God washed it with a flood, hoping to start over. The people demonstrated their selfishness when they built a city and a tower to bind them together instead of spreading out and populating the earth as they had been asked to do.

It is important to remember that on the same day Adam and Eve ate the forbidden fruit, God turned to the enemy and declared that one day a descendant of Adam and Eve's would defeat him. This was a promise they had desperately clung to. Even though the serpent had won a victory in the Garden of Eden, they were encouraged that his victory would only be temporary. One day, someone would defeat him and Satan's work against God would ultimately come to an end.

Who was this descendant who would be able to defeat this serpent? How many generations would it take for him to show up? I would guess that Eve no doubt wondered if her first child was the one. Or maybe her second? Or the third? Maybe a grandchild or even a great grandchild! Who would be the one to have the power to give the enemy of God such a decisive blow that it would destroy him?

That promised one had not been born yet by the time of the flood, as the world was only eight people short of being totally evil and rebellious against God. He had not been born yet by the time the nations dispersed and began to scatter out across the earth from the Tower of Babel. No one had yet been identified as the one to accomplish this significant task.

Everything that had happened so far sets the stage for what comes next. In essence God is saying, "the world is completely broken, and I will fix it." We get to watch as He begins the process of rescuing the world.

We start by zeroing in on one man and his family. God personally chose a man for the task of being the patriarch of the nation from whom this savior, the one who would defeat the enemy, would eventually be born.

The man's name was Abram. What would it be like to be hand-picked by God for a special task? What was it about his character that qualified him for the purpose God had in mind? Just like Noah, there must have been something about Abram that made him stand out in spiritual contrast to the world in which he lived.

God spoke to Abram directly and invited him to take his family, his belongings, and his livestock to permanently relocate to a new home, far away in another country. God didn't even tell him where he was going, just that He would let Abram know when he got there. He would not ever be coming back to live here again.

God then made an amazing promise to Abram. For you to sense the greatness of it all, it is important to quote it directly. "Leave your native country and go to a land that I WILL show you. I WILL make you a great nation. I WILL bless you and make you famous. I WILL bless those who bless you and curse those who treat you with contempt. All the families on earth will be blessed through you." Genesis 12:1-3 (Emphasis mine.)

Did you catch that? Did you notice all the things God said He would do for them? Then the highlight of the promise, "ALL THE FAMILIES ON EARTH will be blessed!" Through Abram's family. That is a breathtaking statement because it includes you and me, four thousand years later. We are members of "all the families on Earth." Every person, individually, would be blessed by the one who would be born as a descendant of Abram. We are now a little closer to identifying the child promised to Adam and Eve who would destroy the enemy and his work. We now know that he would be born from the lineage of Abram.

Imagine Abram coming home after that conversation with God and announcing to his wife Sarai, "Honey, we're moving. We need to have a garage sale and get rid of everything except the photographs, some clothing and those few precious keepsakes from your mother."

"Really! Where are we moving to?"

"I don't know, we just need to hit the road, and God said He would show us when we get there."

What an adventure! How many wives would be excited about that kind of interruption in their life? But she packed up and got ready to go. They lived in a small town known as Ur, in today's Iraq, not far from the Persian Gulf. Abram and Sarai, with a few family members, servants, and livestock headed North, then West, then South again. They ended up in the land that today we know as Israel, but at that time it was called Shechem. At that time it was a land occupied by a variety of tribes of people broadly known as Canaanites.

God told Abram that his travel was done. He had arrived. This would be his new home. Abram built an altar, offered a sacrifice and spent time in worship, expressing his thanks to God. The Canaanite people worshiped many gods, but none included the Creator God that

Abram believed in. Abram's altars were a witness of His faith, and whenever the people came upon an altar, they knew that Abram had already been there.

The promise God had given to Abram had two parts. I will make of you a great nation, and all the families of the earth will be blessed through you. Abram and Sarai had one tiny little challenge with God's promise. In total exasperation, Abram said to God, and I paraphrase, "God, have you noticed, we have a problem on our hands. (Maybe this was the precursor to "Houston, we have a problem!") You promised us a nation of people, out of which someone would be born who would bless all the nations of the earth, but we don't have any children. There's got to be at least one child before there can be a nation. Obviously, this isn't going to happen, so I've got it all figured out and have decided that I will leave all my possessions to my servant."

God assured Abram that His promise was unconditionally guaranteed. Abram would in fact have a son. One night He took Abram outside of the tent he lived in, pointed up to the sky and asked him to count the stars. Well, we all know that is impossible. Then God said to him, "That's how many descendants you will have."

When you don't yet have even one child, that takes a whole boatload of faith to accept! I like what it says next. "Abram believed the LORD, and the LORD counted him as righteous because of his faith." Genesis 15:6. Abram's deep, strong faith must have been what qualified him for this task and for all God wanted to do through him.

Then God gave Abram more detailed information about his family's future. He said, "Your descendants will go and will be strangers in a foreign land." Not only that, He added that they would be slaves in that land for about 400 years, a very long time, but God promised that He would personally rescue them and bring them all back to this land that He was giving to Abram. God concluded by saying that when they left that land where they had been slaves to come back home, they would possess great wealth.

Abram believed God but could not reconcile the things he had been told when in fact he still had no son, not even one. Abram was an old man, and Sarai was well beyond childbearing age. The potential for having a child was long gone. In her despair, Sarai came up with a solution regarding how she would work it out for God, since He obviously wasn't going to be able to fulfill His own promise. Isn't that just like us today? We impulsively think we need to help God work things out so He will be able to fulfill His plan for us.

Sarai excitedly related her brilliant idea to Abram. "My servant Hagar is my possession. Everything she has is mine. Why don't you go to her, have a son with her, and then that son will be mine as well. She can have the son that I cannot, but since she is my servant, and you will be the father, we will just call it the same as me having my own son."

Abram decided that might be a good solution to the dilemma they were facing. Without running the idea past God first, he agreed to participate. Sure enough, Hagar became pregnant, and she had a son. The problem was solved, and they hadn't even needed God. Or so they thought.

In the world of feelings, emotions, and jealousy, and in the midst of a sensitive family drama like this, is it any surprise that Sarai and Hagar began to quarrel? Hagar had given birth to this boy. How was she expected to give up her motherly instincts and pass him over to Sarai? How do two women, a mother and a "wanna-be" mother, navigate that scenario? Hagar had been able to give Abram a child, something that Sarai had never been able to do. There was jealousy and tension everywhere he turned. It was an unpleasant time to live in Abram's camp. I can only guess he took a lot of long walks and when he was home he did a lot of walking on eggshells. Abram learned that helping God out does not always bring a pleasant result. These are the kinds of problems we create when we do things our way instead of God's way.

Hagar's son was named Ishmael, and Abram was 86 years old when he was born. Since Sarai was not the mother, Ishmael was not the child that God had promised they would have together. Thirteen more years went by, and Sarai still had no son of her own.

When Abram was ninety-nine years old, God visited him once again and reminded Abram of His promise. God told Abram that his name would be changed and that he would now be known as Abraham because he was going to be the father of many nations. He added that there would be kings in his family. Then God promised that He was Abraham's God and He would always be the God of his children as well. He promised Abraham that his family would possess this land forever. These were all great words, but there was still no child. Abraham was now very old and Sarai wasn't getting any younger. Naturally, once again he asked, "How can this be?"

I can imagine that Abraham might have been thinking, "I'm not as spry as I used to be! How is a one-hundred-year-old man expected to keep up to a three-year-old toddler! He's going to want to play ball, and I can hardly walk, let alone run with him!

God also told Abraham that Sarai's name would be changed to Sarah, that she would be blessed as well. She would indeed have a son with Abraham, and would be the mother of nations. God repeated the earlier message that kings would be born from among her children.

Abraham responded, probably in amazed frustration, even exasperation, "I'm a hundred years old and Sarah is ninety! You will have to do this through Ishmael." Once again, God assured him that he and Sarah would have a son. Then, things again went frustratingly silent.

Another whole year went by until once again God appeared and said, "I will return to you about this time next year, and your wife, Sarah, will have a son." FINALLY they had a timeline!

Sarah overheard the conversation from inside her tent, laughed to herself, and exclaimed, "How could a worn-out woman like me enjoy such pleasure, especially when my husband is even older than me?"

That's a great question. The LORD heard her question and asked Abraham, "Is anything too hard for the LORD?" What do you think? Is the God who created the world in seven days by the word of His mouth able to make it possible for a very old man and a very old woman to conceive a son? Is anything too hard for God?"

God answered His own question. He proved that He is able to fulfill any promise that He makes. Nothing can stand in His way. He's just that kind of God.

Just as God had said, when He returned a year later, Sarah, even in her old age, had given birth to a son. Sarah laughed again, this time in sheer joy. She was full of laughter, and she named her boy Isaac, which means "He will laugh." Because Isaac was the son promised to Abraham decades ago back in his hometown of Ur, born of Sarah, the promised Savior would be from a descendent of Isaac, not Ishmael.

Once again, the two mothers, Hagar and Sarah, began to experience jealousy and challenges, this time relating to their two boys. Hagar and Ishmael made fun of Isaac and life around camp was tense and anything but pleasant. There was simply too much family drama. Eventually, Sarah had had enough and begged Abraham for help. He was distraught. Ishmael was his son, too. But finally he ended up asking Hagar and Ishmael to move away. They left the camp where they had lived and made a life of their own. Ishmael's descendants became the nations of the Middle East countries as we know them today. His life was blessed because he too was the son of Abraham, but he was not the son God promised would be born to Abraham and Sarah.

You can read all the details in Genesis chapters 12 through 21.

GOD WANTS US TO REMEMBER:

- God, who can see the big picture and always has an eye on the future, prepares us and sets us up for the things that He knows are already in the plan.

- Even when some things, even God's word itself, does not make sense to us, nothing is too hard for God. We can absolutely trust His word, and He will follow through on the promises He makes.

- God does not need our help to fulfill what He has already promised.

- God's timing knows no hurry. While we get impatient when things don't develop on our timeline, God is still leading, and He fully understands what He is doing.

5

GOD WORKS WITH WHAT HE HAS

I'm guessing that it would not surprise you in the least to learn that Isaac was the only child Abraham and Sarah had. After all, Abraham was one hundred and Sarah was ninety when their promised son was finally born. One son was not a sky full of stars, but it was a start. How cherished he must have been.

When Isaac was a teenager, God really tested Abraham's faith. He spoke to Abraham and instructed him to do the unthinkable. In fact, it is so shocking that some don't believe the story at all, saying that God would never ask this of him. Abraham was instructed to take Isaac, his only son, put him on an altar and sacrifice him. Yes! The very son he had waited so many years for. The one who would be the means by which God would fulfill the promise to Abraham that he would be the father of nations. The one Abraham loved so much. Abraham knew God's voice well by now, so as mind-blowing as the message was, he was certain it was a message from God, for him. With a heavy heart, Abraham decided he had no choice but to obey.

Abraham took his son, along with two of his servants and traveled for three days to the place God had instructed him to go. When Abraham saw the mountain in the distance, he asked his servants to wait, took Isaac on alone and continued his journey. As they plodded along together, Isaac asked the obvious question. "Father, we have wood, we have fire, but we don't have a sacrifice!" Abraham's heart pounded as he falteringly answered, "God will provide the sheep for the burnt offering."

Upon arrival at the appointed location, with a questioning, yet hopeful heart, Abraham slowly prepared the altar, no doubt silently pleading for God to intervene. When he could stall no longer, he had no choice but to explain to Isaac what God had asked him to do. The youthful Isaac could have easily overpowered his one-hundred-plus year-old father. Instead, he lay down on the altar, no doubt in fear and confusion, but was willing to die because he trusted his father, who he knew trusted God.

The heart-broken Abraham was ready to sacrifice this promised son although none of this made any sense to him whatsoever. At the last possible moment, a voice spoke to him that arrested the downward thrust of his knife. The message was clear. "Abraham! Abraham! Do not hurt the boy. Lay the knife down. Now I know that you truly do fear God. You did not withhold your only son from me!"

No doubt there must have been a gasp of relief. Likely tears and probably a heartfelt, long hug between father and son. Then, for the first time, Abraham noticed a ram caught in a nearby bush, and that animal became the sacrifice instead. Truly, God had provided a sacrifice, just as Abraham had said to Isaac. This whole event is significant, and I share it because it is a vivid metaphor for the main theme of the whole Bible. We will refer to this story again later.

When Isaac was old enough to be married, Abraham sent his trusted servant, (we are not told his name) back to his homeland to find a suitable mate for him. His one requirement for Isaac was that he would be married to someone who believed in the same Creator God as he and his family. The people among whom they currently lived did not share a belief in that God at all.

The servant traveled the many dusty miles all the way back to the homeland where Abraham had come from. He had many wearisome miles to consider exactly how he would go about picking out the right woman for Isaac, the one who would become his wife. He didn't feel confident to make that decision on his own so asked God for some simple indicator that would assure him he had found the right wife for Isaac. It was decided the sign would be that the woman who offered him a refreshing drink of water as well as enough for his thirsty camels would be the one he was to invite to travel back home with him.

Sure enough! The script unfolded perfectly. As he sat in the shade to rest after his hot, dusty journey, a young lady named Rebekah came to the well. He asked her for a drink which she happily offered. Then she quickly began to draw water for all his camels as well. Not a small task, I am sure.

When the servant explained his mission to Rebekah's father, and that she had perfectly met the details of the sign he had asked God for, the family was speechless. Turning to her, they asked her if she was willing to go. Without hesitation, she assured them that she was. Think of the mind and heart of this brave young woman as she started off to a far country with a stranger; to marry a man the servant had only described to her.

Picture Isaac walking in the fields back at home, praying and wondering how things were going. How his pulse must have raced when he first saw the servant's camels and entourage arriving back home. There was no courtship. There was no big wedding. When the servant said the man coming toward them was his master and her husband to be, Rebekah covered her face, and after whatever marriage customs they followed, she became Isaac's wife. All we are told is that "he loved her deeply."

Since Abraham had only one promised son with Sarah, it was obviously up to Isaac to provide the promised lineage for Abraham. Isaac and Rebekah doubled the number of children Abraham had been promised when they gave birth to twin sons, naming them Esau and Jacob.

Esau was the older son with Jacob being born a few minutes later. The traditional and expected family ritual was that when the firstborn son came to the right age, his father would bestow inheritance blessings on him, called the birthright.

When the time came to honor Esau in this way, Isaac asked him to go hunting and prepare a meal, after which he would then bestow upon him the birthright blessings. Rebekah overheard the conversation and hurriedly sprang into action. Of the two boys, she favored Jacob and wanted him to receive the blessing, so she set out to get her way. Like Sarah, she was determined to help God out since this was not going to turn out "the right way" if she didn't. The human heart often determines to just do things our own way because we are not convinced that God can be trusted to do it right.

She quickly began preparing a meal and suggested to Jacob that he put on Esau's clothing so that he would smell like Esau, and animal skins on his arms to pretend that he was hairy, like Esau. Jacob was smooth skinned, unlike Esau. Isaac was getting older, going blind, and it was hoped these preparations would be enough to pull off this fateful trick.

The ruse went perfectly. Isaac felt Jacob's arms, smelled his clothing, and was mystified that it seemed like Esau, but the voice sounded like Jacob. Isaac enjoyed the meal, complimented him on finding it so quickly, and then prayed the family blessing over him. Knowing exactly what he had done, Jacob quickly left his father's presence in the nick of time as just then Esau appeared with his prepared meal. Isaac was so horrified that he sat trembling when he realized that he had been tricked and that he had already given the birthright blessing to Jacob.

Esau begged for a blessing for himself, but Isaac said he could not take it back. Esau was so angry that his parents were afraid he may kill Jacob, so they decided to send Jacob back to their homeland, where Abraham, Sarah, and Rebekah had come from. There he would be safe. They also hoped that he would find a wife there. Isaac blessed Jacob again and sent him on his journey. Jacob never did see his mother again because she died before he returned.

Jacob spent a lot of time alone as he traveled. He had the family blessing, but he did not have the blessing of a family at this time. As Jacob slept on the very first night of his journey, he had a most amazing dream where he saw a ladder that reached all the way from Earth to Heaven, covered with angels. He watched the angels going up to Heaven and then back down to the earth again on that ladder. Then he noticed God Himself standing at the top of the ladder, who spoke directly to Jacob.

"I am the God of your grandfather Abraham, and the God of your father Isaac." Then, in what was becoming a habit for God, He repeated the promise that had been made to Abraham, then to Isaac, and now personally to Jacob. God told him that the land he was laying on would belong to him and his entire offspring. God promised Jacob that his descendants would be like the dust of the earth who would spread out in all directions on the planet. And then came those same promised words once again, only this time given to the grandson of Abraham. "All the families of the earth will be blessed through you and your descendants." This part of the promise must have been important to God because He kept repeating it to each new generation.

Jacob traveled to the land of his mother's family and began to work as a shepherd. He quickly noticed and fell in love with a young woman named Rachel. He was so in love with her that she was a total distraction to him. He negotiated his wages with Rachel's father, Laban, who promised Jacob that he could marry her if he worked for him for seven years. Jacob was so starstruck by Rachel that the years were nothing to him, and it seemed but just a few days until the time was up. He was giddy with excitement as the time came that he could finally marry the love of his heart.

On the wedding night, Laban tricked Jacob by bringing Rachel's older sister, Leah, to his tent. Wearing a veil and staying silent, Jacob was none the wiser. When Jacob saw her clearly in the morning light and realized that it was not Rachel, he understandably exploded in anger at her father. We would probably all agree that his anger was justified. He didn't want to marry Leah; he had worked all these years to marry Rachel. Laban's feeble excuse was that he could not give the younger sister to be married while the older sister was still single.

Jacob was then allowed to marry Rachel also, but only after a week of marriage celebration for Leah. Also, Laban gave Rachel to Jacob on the condition that he work another seven years, which he agreed to do because he loved her so much. This is not the textbook way to get a father and son-in-law relationship off to a healthy start.

What follows next could easily fill a good-sized paperback or become the storyline plot of an ongoing afternoon TV soap opera!

Jacob was tricked into marrying Leah, but he loved Rachel. That's a perfect setting in which to percolate an intense case of sibling rivalry. To make matters worse, Leah quickly had a son, and then another one. Sons three and four followed in rapid succession. Rachel on the other hand was not able to conceive at all, making it easy to pile up deep anger and resentment toward her sister. She complained bitterly to anyone who would listen, and no doubt had a few choice words for Jacob about why she had no children at all. Jacob could only take so much of her weeping and begging and reminded her in exasperation that he was not God who had control over when babies would be conceived. I'm guessing some days it was probably just easier for Jacob to spend a lot of time out on the hills watching the sheep.

Rachel then stole a page out of Sarah's and Abraham's playbook. She encouraged Jacob to have children with her servant, Bilhah, who gave Jacob two sons. Now Rachel could at least imagine that she had two sons, but still lived in sadness because she was not yet a satisfied mother herself.

Leah had stopped having children, so she gave Jacob her servant, Zilpah, who also gave Jacob two sons. Then Leah had two more sons. All this time, Rachel was still waiting, no doubt weeping, hurting, angry and jealous. She was running out of child-bearing years.

If you are counting, Leah now had six sons. Bilhah had two sons. Zilpah had two sons. Ten in total, and Rachel was still waiting in desperation. How many nights did she flood her pillow with tears, and shake her clenched fist at God and at Jacob?

And some think the Bible is boring! If you sat down in a room full of writers you couldn't make up a more twisted, complicated plot. Here they all lived in a family camp, full of siblings, many of them close to each other in age.

Finally, Rachel ecstatically gave birth to a son, naming him Joseph. He was the son of her dreams, and Jacob finally now had a son with the one woman he truly loved. To throw a little fuel on the emotional level of the family drama, the way Jacob doted over this boy made it abundantly clear that Joseph was his favorite child.

Rachel then had one more son, Benjamin. Jacob's family was now complete. Twelve sons, and Leah also had one daughter mentioned as well.

Eventually the family returned home to the land that God had given to Abraham and had promised to Jacob while standing on the ladder in the dream. Jacob and Esau patched things up and the family that was to become more than the sands of the seashore was beginning to come into focus. The twelve sons grew up, married, and had children of their own. Just as God had changed Abram's name to Abraham, He now changed Jacob's name to Israel. All the families of the twelve sons collectively became known as the Children of Israel.

Jacob could not contain the joy he experienced over the fact that he and Rachel had finally given birth to a son and continued to make it no secret that Joseph was his pet. Jacob made a flashy, expensive, multi-colored coat, just for Joseph, but never prepared anything remotely like it for the other eleven sons.

One day, Jacob asked Joseph to go on a short journey to check on his brothers who were away pasturing their sheep. This was an adventure any boy would be happy to go on so Joseph excitedly packed up and headed out on his way.

When the brothers saw him coming to them, wearing his bright coat, jealousy got the better of them. They had put up with this "spoiled brat" long enough. They were not prepared for him to show up and did not have any plan as to what they should do with him, so they simply grabbed Joseph and threw him down into a nearby pit to wait while they talked it over. Then suddenly the answer came to them! A band of merchandise traders passed by on their way to Egypt. The brothers grabbed Joseph, tore off the precious coat and sold him as a slave. It was a tough day for a boy who was just out to obey his father and see his brothers, expecting they would be happy to see him.

The brothers then took the coat, dipped it in animal blood and carried it to their father, tricking him into believing that Joseph had been killed by some wild beast. Jacob wailed out in grief with a sound that was no doubt heard by everyone in the camp. "I will go to my death mourning my son," he cried. What must it have been like for those brothers to hear his weeping and experience their father's grief and anguish every day, all the time knowing that his grief was due only to their actions and lies?

When Joseph arrived wide-eyed and terrified in Egypt, he was sold to a man named Potiphar, the officer in charge of the security detail for Pharaoh, king of Egypt. Joseph worked so diligently and with such integrity for Potiphar, that he was easily trusted and quickly put in charge of his entire household.

Potiphar's wife relentlessly attempted to entice Joseph into a relationship that could only be described as a sinful indiscretion. Angry that he continually refused her advances, one day she grabbed at him. As he bolted his coat came off in her hands. She screamed out, accusing him of trying to assault her, using his coat as evidence. It was she who had acted inappropriately, but as a woman scorned, she was out for revenge. Joseph was charged and thrown into prison.

Life was not going well for Joseph. He had been sold by his brothers because of jealousy. Now, he had been falsely accused and thrown into prison when he had in fact demonstrated integrity and unwavering loyalty to Potipher as well as to his own values. We could not blame Joseph if he cried out to God, "Why do these things keep happening to me? I am simply going about life the best way I know how!" When life doesn't feel fair to us, we can remember Joseph and take comfort in the fact that Bible characters experience the same heartache and losses that we feel. That's why their lives can be such an encouragement to us.

Joseph's character did not go unnoticed, even in prison. He was soon put in charge of the other prisoners along with everything that happened there. One day, two of King Pharaoh's high officials were thrown into prison for something that had obviously been offensive to the king. One was the king's cupbearer, and the other was the king's baker. Joseph soon became acquainted with them.

One morning Joseph noticed that they seemed troubled, so he inquired about it. They told him that each of them had a significant dream the night before, but they had no idea what the dreams meant. When they told Joseph the dreams, God gave Joseph insight into what the dreams meant. He had good news for the cupbearer and said that in three days he would be restored to his position in the palace. Then, he sadly told the baker that the news was not as good for him, and in three days he in fact would be executed. Joseph then turned to the cupbearer pleading with him to explain to Pharoah that he had been sold as a slave back in his homeland and that he had done nothing wrong to bring about a jail sentence. He was simply seeking justice. The cupbearer promised that he would in fact deliver the message as requested.

Both dreams came true exactly as Joseph said, but in his excitement of reinstatement, the cupbearer forgot to talk to the king about Joseph. Well, that is until one night Pharaoh himself had two very troubling dreams and wanted to know what they meant. Suddenly, the cupbearer remembered Joseph, the interpreter of dreams, who was quickly summoned to the palace to speak to the king. This was the turn of events Joseph had been hoping for.

Once again, Joseph did not have the wisdom inside of himself to give an answer, but God enabled him to interpret the dreams for the king. Joseph explained to Pharaoh that the message was clear. The dreams meant that Egypt was going to experience seven years of incredible, bountiful harvests of grain, unlike anything they had ever known. Then, in a complete reversal, the seven years of abundant harvest would be immediately followed by seven years of drought and famine, also unlike anything they had ever known.

Egypt was about to face an economic nightmare that no ruler ever wants to have to deal with. Joseph went on to suggest that they should build many storage places, collect the grain from these first bountiful years in order to be able to feed the people who would surely be in need during the seven years of famine. The plan was so incredibly wise that Pharaoh appointed Joseph, on the spot, to manage the whole program. In the incredible turn of events, within a few short hours, Joseph was not only free from prison, but he was also now second in command and answered only to the king in all the land of Egypt.

Exactly as predicted, the seven years of bumper crops began. The storage facilities were built, and the grain was carefully stored. Then, also as predicted, the seven prosperous years ended, and the devastating famine began. Months grew into years when no grain was harvested, and the nation was grateful for the wisdom of Joseph and the preparations he had made.

Back home in Israel where his family lived, the famine began to take its toll there as well. Joseph's brothers and father found themselves in need of grain for food for their families and their livestock. The news reached them that there was grain in Egypt, so some of the brothers made the trip to buy grain. The day none of them expected had finally come. Joseph was about to meet his dishonest and abusive brothers once again, face to face. Of course, they would not even remotely expect Joseph to be involved in their business transaction of buying grain. At best, they could only picture him to no doubt be serving someone as a slave somewhere. Even in their wildest dreams they would never picture him to be assistant to the king of Egypt.

What follows is a series of events that is one of the favorite stories in the Bible. Joseph's excitement at seeing his brothers was tempered by his wisdom. He withheld his eagerness because he wanted to test his brothers to see if they were still the mean-spirited men they had been the day they sold him to slave traders. He accused them of being spies, but they protested that they were all brothers of one man, who had already lost a son, and there was still a younger son at home. Joseph continued to charge them as spies.

Finally, he kept one brother prisoner and insisted that they bring the younger brother next time to prove they were telling the truth.

After they had purchased their grain, Joseph directed his servants to put their money back into their sacks of grain. As they stopped for the night one of them found the money in his sack. They were deeply confused about these strange series of events.

When they arrived home, each found their money in their grain bags! They were speechless, in fact terrified. They had been accused of spying, now they could be accused as thieves as well. They filled Jacob in on all the strange events that had unfolded in Egypt. Then they told Jacob that "the man" had said that their brother Simeon would only be released when they went back on the condition that Benjamin went along with them. Jacob was terrified of losing Rachel's second son and vowed it would be impossible. Benjamin would never be allowed to go to Egypt.

Eventually, the family again ran out of grain and knew that it was time to go back to Egypt once again. They reminded Jacob that their youngest brother must go along, or the trip would be futile. Reluctantly, Jacob admitted that he had no choice and gave permission for Benjamin to go.

Joseph was deeply moved to see his younger brother again. He decided to test them all one more time. When they were ready to go back home with their grain, Joseph had one of his servants put his own personal golden goblet in Benjamin's grain bag. After they had been on the road home for a time, Joseph's men caught up to the brothers and asked why they had stolen the cup. The brothers were adamant that they would never do such a thing. They were so sure that they did not have the cup that they promised that the one who had it would stay as a prisoner in Egypt.

Imagine their sickening shock and panic when the cup was found in Benjamin's bag.

Upon arrival back in Egypt, one of the older brothers begged Joseph to let him stay in prison instead of Benjamin because their father would be too distraught. He told Joseph that his father had lost one son already and would surely die if he lost the second one. Joseph could contain himself no longer. This was what he had been watching for and it was now clear that these brothers were changed from the men who had sold him into slavery. He asked all his servants to leave the room and then he broke down and wept so loudly the people out on the streets could hear him. They must have wondered about such an emotional outburst from this mighty ruler in Egypt.

Finally, he gathered his composure and introduced himself. "I am Joseph, your brother who you sold into slavery. Do not blame yourselves, God sent me here ahead of you so that I could prepare and care for you at this time. Quick, go back and tell my father I am still alive. Get him and bring him and all your families to Egypt. The famine is not yet over, and I will care for you here."

As each tongue-tied brother tried to find something to say, I can imagine that the best they could offer was a stuttering, incoherent response. Filled with panic, they realized that Joseph now had the firm upper hand on them and could take out his revenge on them any way he chose to. Joseph assured them there would be no retaliation or payback. They were safe and he wanted them all to come to live in Egypt near to him. He sent extra carts and wagons to help facilitate the move of the entire family.

I wonder about the thoughts they must have had as the brothers arrived to confess to their father that they had lied to him all those years ago. They informed him that Joseph was still alive, and it was they who had sold him as a slave. What must it have been like to now be accountable for the years of grief their father had experienced?

At first Jacob didn't believe them, but when they showed him all the wagons Joseph had sent to bring their families to Egypt, he quickly got ready to go. I'm guessing he may have laughed and sang all the way to Egypt, making up for the years of grief. Once again, he would be reunited with Joseph before he died. It was the Best-Day-Ever for Jacob.

When Joseph was informed the family was almost in Egypt, he went out to meet them. What an emotional day that must have been for Jacob as he once again hugged his beloved, favorite son. They were finally all together when no one ever thought that would be possible. Joseph saw to it that they were given the very best of the land where there was pasture to care for their livestock. This was new as farming was not a typical Egyptian occupation. Jacob's family was now living in a foreign land.

Jacob died in Egypt, as did Joseph, and all the brothers, along with several generations of their offspring. Joseph had given strict instructions that his bones be carried back to his father's homeland and buried there.

We remember that God had told Abraham his descendants would be "strangers in a foreign land." He added that they would be slaves there for about four hundred years. God promised that He would personally rescue them and bring them all back to the land that He had given to Abraham. Here they were, now strangers in a foreign land. The word of God was being fulfilled exactly as He said it would.

The unfolding story of Abraham's family is tumultuous. The drama, the deceit, the family chaos was all chronicled in full and sometimes uncomplimentary detail for us to read for ourselves. God loves us and still uses us for His plans despite our broken human condition. He continually works to bring out the good that He wants to accomplish, even when we don't make it easy for Him to do so.

You can read all the details of these events in Genesis chapters 22 through 50.

GOD WANTS US TO REMEMBER:

- When life events happen that do not make sense to us, God may be doing a special work within us in order to strengthen our faith and prepare us for important events in the future.

- Abraham, Sarah, and then Rebekah and Jacob went about taking matters into their own hands to help God accomplish what they were afraid He would not or could not do on His own. The consequences of those actions often brought suffering along with them. When we simply trust Him, God is free to do amazing and miraculous things on our behalf.

- Joseph suffered much at the hands of others, but bitterness never seemed to overtake his heart and mind. In the end he could see, and stated to his brothers, that God was in fact preparing the way to be able to take care of his family when it would be necessary. He could see a good news story through it all. Perspective about God makes a tremendous difference in our understanding of His role in our lives.

6

THE LONG AND WINDING ROAD

Exactly as God had predicted, Jacob's offspring were now strangers in a foreign land. The number of descendants of Jacob increased at an astonishing rate. God had prophesied they would be like the sand of the seashore or the stars in the heavens and it soon became evident that Egypt had two nations of people within its borders.

The small cluster of Abraham's immediate family were known as the Hebrews. God had changed Jacob's name to Israel, so his family became known as the Children of Israel, or Israelites. The Hebrews were simply ancestors of the Israelites. The terms Hebrews, Israelites, and the Children of Israel are often interchanged but all refer to Abraham's family and their lineage at different reference points through the years and centuries since.

Decades went by and eventually the name and memory of Joseph had no further impact on life in Egypt. A Pharaoh, who knew nothing about Joseph, came to the throne and expressed concern about the extensive growth of this foreign tribe of people who occupied so much of his territory.

Thinking strategically, this Pharaoh decided it would be wise to flex his authority, eventually forcing the whole nation of Hebrew people into slavery. Pharaoh after Pharaoh kept them enslaved and used their hard labor to build the infrastructure of the nation of Egypt. The people were compelled to make bricks and then use those same bricks to build cities for him. The work was hot, back breaking and never-ending. God had correctly told Abraham that they would live in a foreign land for a period of about four hundred years, spending many of those years as slaves. It was all playing out exactly as He had said it would.

Centuries after Joseph's family had originally moved to Egypt, one of the Pharaohs took his dictatorial authority to a whole new level. He decreed that along with the drudgery of slavery, the Hebrew midwives were to immediately kill any male Hebrew child at the time it was born. He added this disgusting requirement to take away any opportunity for someone to be born who would become a leader who could possibly start a revolt by which the Hebrew people would overpower Egypt.

The midwives would not follow such a horrific request, and Pharaoh called them in for accountability. The answer was simple. "The Hebrew women give birth so quickly we don't get there in time." So, what does a bully do then? Pharaoh put it out to all Egyptian people that they were to cast all baby boys born to the Hebrews into the river. Instead of a celebration and time of joy, it would be terrifying for a young family to find out they were going to have another baby.

One mother, named Jochebed, (Yawk-eh-bed) sensing that she had given birth to a special child, was so determined to save her boy that she kept him hidden, but was fully aware that it was only a matter of time until he would surely be detected. Hiding him much longer was going to be impossible. She constructed a basket of papyrus reeds, made it waterproof, placed her baby in it, and put the basket in the water among the bullrushes along the bank of the Nile River. The baby's older sister, Miriam, was stationed nearby to guard the basket.

As was her practice, the palace princess, daughter of Pharaoh, came to the river to bathe. She noticed the basket, looked inside and her heart melted at the cute smile that little boy flashed as she opened the lid. Taking in the scene she realized that a Hebrew mother was attempting to keep her child safe from her father's horrific edict. Miriam quickly appeared, offering to find a nurse for the baby. When the princess agreed, Miriam breathlessly ran to get her mother.

Jochebed and the princess arrived at an agreement that would preserve the baby's life. The princess would pay Jochebed to care for her own son and assured her that he would be safe. Then when he was older, the princess would come to get him, and he would live in the palace with her.

Jochebed became fully aware that she had just a few short years to implant into her child's mind the principles of faith and trust in God she wanted him to learn. At the agreed upon time, Jochebed took him to Pharaoh's daughter, who adopted him and named him Moses, because, "I lifted him out of the water." Moses left his Hebrew family and went to the palace to experience life among royalty. He would now study Egyptian life and spirituality, philosophy, war, leadership and live the life of a prince.

When he was about forty years of age, Moses came across an Egyptian who was beating one of the Hebrew slaves. He knew his heritage, and this was so upsetting to Moses that after looking in all directions first, he killed the Egyptian and buried his body in the sand. The very next day, he came across two Hebrew men fighting, so he tried to stop the argument. One of them sneered at him and asked, "Who appointed you prince and judge over us? Are you going to kill me like you killed that Egyptian yesterday?" Can you hear the oxygen leaving Moses lungs as he sharply exhaled?

Moses' blood ran cold as he realized his deed was known and feared that Pharaoh would hear about it. Sure enough, Pharaoh did find out and tried to kill Moses. Moses accepted the fact that his life here would be in danger forever, so he quietly slipped out of town as a fugitive, leaving Egypt for good. Searching for a place of safety he arrived in Midian, far from all the trouble back home, determined to hide and enjoy a fresh start. Midian is thought to have been what we would know to be Southern Judea today.

Moses met a desert-dweller named Jethro, who gave him work as a shepherd, something he would have no knowledge of or experience with. Moses must have been pleased to discover that Jethro also had

WHAT IF IT'S TRUE?

daughters. He married Zipporah, had two sons, peacefully settling into the quiet life of a shepherd, far away from his birth family, the palace, and the threat of the king back in Egypt. For the next forty years, Moses wandered the desert with his sheep, always searching for food and water for their well-being, learning the lessons of life that only the wilderness could teach him.

The now eighty-year-old Moses must have been having thoughts of retirement and settling down in a tent somewhere in the shade, overlooking a cool oasis for the rest of his life. However, that dream was completely interrupted one day when he noticed a strange phenomenon. There in the desert, all by itself, was a bush on fire. However, the fascinating thing that got his attention was that as he watched the bush burn, the bush did not burn up. He decided to become the Sherlock Holmes of the desert and investigate this strange sight.

As he got closer, he heard a voice speaking to him. "Moses! Moses! Don't come any closer. Take your sandals off, you are standing on holy ground. I am the God of your father, the God of Abraham, the God of Isaac, and the God of Jacob." Moses started to tremble. He was in the presence of God himself, listening to His voice. Here is an example of a mere mortal not feeling safe in the presence of a Holy God. (A little more electricity than Moses was comfortable with.) In reverence, he quickly removed his shoes and covered his face. He was afraid to look at God. There he stood, waiting to find out what would happen next.

God informed Moses that He wanted him to go back to Egypt to finally deliver His people from their slavery. It was time for God to take Jacob's family home. Back to the land He had promised to Abraham, and to Isaac. Back to the land where Jacob and his family had been living when Joseph relocated them to Egypt.

I can imagine that once again Moses had a hard time catching his breath. The thought of going back to Egypt where there had been a bounty on his head was terrifying. When his tongue finally began to work again, he came up with what he thought were four great reasons why God had asked the wrong man.

Moses was forty years removed from anything other than family and sheep. His lack of confidence brought forth the question, "Who am I that I should appear before Pharaoh?" God said, "I'll be with you. You won't have to go do this alone."

Moses protested, "They aren't going to believe me. If I tell them the God of their ancestors sent me, they are going to ask me what His name is. What do I say then?" God replied, "I AM WHO I AM. Say this to the people of Israel: I AM has sent me to you. . . . The God of Abraham, the God of Isaac, and the God of Jacob has sent me to you." Exodus 3:14,15

Moses continued his resistance. "They won't believe me. They won't do what I tell them. They are just going to say, 'The LORD never appeared to you.'" God replied, "What do you have there in your hand?" "A shepherd's staff," said Moses. "Throw it on the ground," the LORD said, so Moses did. Immediately the staff became a snake from which a terrified Moses turned and ran!

Then God said, "Pick it up by the tail." When he did, the snake became a wooden rod again. God added, "Perform this sign, and they will believe you." No doubt God had Moses' attention by now, but his fear was about to crush him.

Finally, in desperation, Moses said, "I get tongue-tied and don't speak well. This is never going to work!" God simply said, "Who made your mouth? I'll teach you what you should say." Then God told him that his brother Aaron would meet him and would be the spokesperson when they confronted Pharaoh. Moses was out of excuses, so reluctantly he agreed to go and carry out God's mission. God told Moses that all those in Egypt who had wanted to kill him forty years earlier were now dead and there was nothing to fear back there.

With Jethro's blessing, Moses took his wife and sons and headed for Egypt. There in the desert, near the mountain where he had met God at the burning bush, Moses and Aaron found each other. God must have been directing their GPS devices with impeccable accuracy so that their paths would cross in that vast wilderness.

Together they went back to see Pharaoh in the palace that Moses knew so well. They told him that the Creator God of Heaven had sent them to ask for the freedom of the Hebrew people. Pharoah scoffed and his arrogance came through as he retorted, "And who is the LORD? Why should I listen to him and let Israel go? I don't know the LORD and I will not let Israel go." The response from God let Pharaoh know exactly who He was with more evidence than Pharaoh bargained for.

Pharaoh soon learned that the God of Moses and Aaron was far more powerful than all the myriad of Egyptian gods together. The events of the next few days and weeks completely devastated the nation of Egypt, all because the king was stubbornly determined to be right and fight the God of Abraham, Isaac, and Jacob. A series of ten destructive plagues hit the land of Egypt in a demonstration of divine power that had never been experienced before, or since.

The first event saw all their water sources turn to blood for a time. Then frogs appeared everywhere. On the streets, in the houses, in the cupboards and even in the beds. In desperation, Pharaoh promised that if the frogs were no more, the people could go. But as soon as the frogs were gone, Pharaoh changed his mind. This was the beginning of a toxic, cyclical pattern. With each plague he would make a promise to finally let the people go, only to then backtrack on those promises once the plague ended.

In quick succession, the nation had to deal with a series of ravaging events, including an infestation of gnats, and then flies. A sickness that affected all their cattle was followed by boils on the people, hail, locusts, then days of dense darkness so thick that no one moved. Finally, the last was the worst one of all. Moses and Aaron announced that from Pharaoh's palace down to the humblest servant's cottage, on a given night at midnight, a death-angel would come over the land and the oldest child in each family would die.

On the night of that final, horrible plague, the Hebrew people were instructed to very carefully perform a ritual that would protect their children and families from the death of their first-born child. They were told to choose a perfect, healthy lamb to sacrifice. Not one that was sick or diseased or broken. They were to then take the blood of that lamb and splash it on the two sides and top of the doorway into their home. Anyone living in a home with blood on the doorposts would be safe. When the angel was doing his dark work, wherever he would find blood on the doorposts, the plague of death would pass over that home. From that night on, every year right down until today, the Hebrew people continue to celebrate the Passover festival, remembering the night that the death angel "passed over" their home because of the blood on the doorposts.

King Pharaoh and his entire nation of people had endured all they could handle and were willing to do whatever it took to end the turmoil. The Egyptian people urged the Hebrew slaves to leave quickly, offering them gold, jewels, and expensive items, all in the hopes that they would just be gone and never return. They wanted their country to begin to return to normal. It was the night of their freedom from slavery. Not only had God told Abraham that they would be freed, He also told them they would leave the land very rich. Exactly as He said, payday finally came for all the work they had done. Egypt was stripped of its riches that night.

It is estimated there may have been as many as two million men, women, and children in that massive crowd of people as they started the journey back to their homeland. They found ways to load up and carry the most essential items, as well as gather their cattle, sheep and whatever essentials they deemed to be necessary.

Speed would not play out in any part of this picture. Daily, this horde of people inched along toward the land they would call home. Within a few days they were camped beside the Red Sea. The sense of adventure was keen, and they could only imagine what might lie ahead. I wonder if their arms were black and blue from pinching themselves, checking to see if they were dreaming or if it indeed was true that they were no longer slaves. God had delivered them, and through the work of Moses and Aaron they were now free!

Back in Egypt, King Pharaoh was once again questioning his decision. As he calculated the loss these slaves would be to his economy, in his rage he decided that he had made a terrible mistake to let the people leave. How short his memory was. He rallied his fighting men and with all the force he had left he headed out on a mission to bring his slaves back. How many of those soldiers wished that he would just leave well enough alone after all they had been through in the last weeks? But they no doubt knew better than to question his actions and simply went along.

The Hebrew people's joy and happiness turned to panic as the word spread that the cloud of dust rising behind them on the horizon was actually the armies of Egypt charging after them in hot pursuit. They were helplessly trapped by the sea and mountains as they heard the pounding horses approaching. The panicked crowd wailed at Moses, reminding him that they would rather be slaves in Egypt than to die here by the sea. It was total chaos!

Moses did not believe for a moment that God had brought them out of slavery in Egypt to this place just to have them die here. He encouraged them to watch to see what God would do for them. Then Moses raised the staff that he had taken with him from the wilderness and held it out over the water. In what is arguably the greatest miracle of the Old Testament, the Red Sea parted, and an escape route was made available for the people to scramble through on dry ground to a place of safety on the other side.

I wonder what courage it would take and who would be the first to walk between those walls of water, and get the whole process started? It was the only option they had, so they charged forward. Eventually, every person and creature were safely on the other side. The Egyptian army had been stopped by an incredible darkness which had settled over them, making it impossible to move forward.

When the darkness eventually lifted, the army realized the people had disappeared and saw the opening in the sea right in front of them. The soldiers riding horses and chariots rushed into the channel after them. It seems odd that after so much supernatural activity which had recently happened to them that Pharaoh would not pause even for a moment at the scene before him. The darkness they had just experienced was not natural, even mysterious. Did the thought never enter his head that said, "Nothing about this is normal? In fact, nothing has been normal for several weeks now. Maybe we should just go back home?" But rage does crazy things and without thinking it through carefully they blindly rushed into the open channel feeling like they were within the very grasp of victory. When they were well out into the middle of the path through the sea, the water closed up again and crashed down upon them. The entire Egyptian army was destroyed in the Red Sea that day.

Finally! There was no question about it now. The Children of Israel were truly free! They would never have to worry about their slave masters or the army of Egypt ever again. They broke out in a song of worship to the God who had now fully secured their freedom.

As they turned their back on the sea to continue toward their homeland, the adventures of Israel in the wilderness were just beginning. What follows is an insight into the care and attention God poured out on His people as He worked to set the foundation for a solid, two-way relationship with them.

No doubt, the first anxious question would be where they would find enough food and water for that many people and animals? God told Moses to strike a rock with his staff and miraculously, water gushed forth in abundance, providing enough to nourish the nation of people, and all the flocks of animals with them.

Along with the fresh water from the rock, every morning there was a white frosting-like substance on the ground called Manna. It was the daily ration of food they were given to eat that would sustain them. It melted away when the sun came up to warm the ground so someone from each family would have to get up early to gather enough for the day. For protection from the elements, God created a cloud to give them shade by day, and a pillar of fire each evening to warm them during the cold desert nights.

Even though God had developed an intimate and personal relationship with their ancestors, Abraham, Isaac and Jacob, these people, recently freed from the bondage of slavery by His miraculous intervention, did not have a close bond with Him. They had been in a land where worship of the Creator God was foreign to their thinking. They had not been allowed to learn of Him and had no concept of who He was or what He was like. Now that God had them in a quiet and safe place, it was His desire to teach them many facets of truth about Himself. He wanted them to know that He was not only a powerful, earth-shaking kind of God, but He was also an ever-present friend. He wanted them to know His heart as well as His power, and to have an intimate, personal relationship with them.

Their journey brought them to Mount Sinai. While they camped there, God chose to speak directly to them from a cloud on the mountain where they could hear Him but would not be able to see Him. He was reducing His might and power to a level in which they would be more readily able to receive Him.

God began by emphasizing His saving relationship with them, and then He presented ten encompassing principles that would forever guide His people on how to live a meaningful life. The first four were designed to teach them how to reverently relate to God, and the following six taught them how to respectfully live in community with each other. Today we refer to them as the Ten Commandments. The values and wisdom presented on that mountain centuries ago are still God's best description of what a full and blessed life looks like. When we follow them, we are at peace with God, with ourselves, and with all people.

God introduced Himself by saying, "I am the LORD your God, who rescued you from the land of Egypt, the place of your slavery."

Then He added:

1. Do not worship other gods. (There is only one Creator God)

2. Do not make idols of wood or stone. (I am able to personally love you where they cannot)

3. Do not misuse or abuse my name. (I am holy, and reverence for my name is appropriate)

4. Remember the Sabbath day to keep it holy. (Honor the time I have set aside for enhancing our relationship)

5. Honor your father and mother. (Respect family)

6. Do not commit murder. (Respect the life of others)

7. Do not commit adultery. (Respect the sacredness of marriage)

8. Do not steal. (Respect the property of others)

9. Do not lie about another person. (Respect truth always)

10. Do not covet your neighbors' goods. (Learn to be at peace and content with what we have)

The people were terrified at the presence of this God. The mountain shook and His voice sounded like thunder. They realized that His divine power was different from any god they had ever experienced. He was holy. He was powerful. With trembling voices, they promised to keep these principles forever.

Along with the Ten Commandments, God also gave Moses pages of instructions on how to live together as a community. These were more local in nature and included things such as what to eat for food, cleanliness, and how to govern the camp. They were instructed in relationships, protection of property and all manner of social and civil community issues.

The details of the rules laid out in the books of Exodus and Leviticus can be a bit mind-numbing. However, when we look at the principles behind the rules instead of just the details, we realize they are full of wisdom and truth, designed to lead these nomadic people to better health, a thriving community, and most importantly, a solid relationship with God Himself. The principles are still valid even today.

Moses was also given detailed instructions on how to build a place for worship. It was called a sanctuary. God told Moses He wanted to dwell among them, and even out here in the desert He wanted a specific location in which to make His presence experienced, felt and honored.

The book of Leviticus spells out a meticulous set of details on when and how the people were to bring seven different types of offerings to this sanctuary. There are also guidelines on specific rituals of how to celebrate seven types of feasts each calendar year. This is usually where people's eyes begin to glaze over as they read the Bible. All the celebrations and offerings they were instructed to follow were for the purpose of understanding how these rituals would enhance their relationship with and their understanding of Him. He truly wanted to be their God and for them to be His people because it was through this chosen family that He wanted to bless the whole earth. He had a specific work to do through them and He wanted them to know Him personally.

Eventually they moved on from Mt. Sinai, and when they arrived at the border of the promised land, they decided to send in twelve spies, asking them to come back with a report as to what they could expect when they settled in. One man was selected from each family, or tribe, of Jacob's twelve sons and with well wishes they were sent on their journey. What would they learn about their new home? Who doesn't like a good spy adventure?

The spies were gone for forty days. When they returned, the people eagerly gathered around and listened as they reported that they had both good news and bad news. The good news was that the land was better than any of them had even dreamed of. It truly was a garden. They called it a land "flowing with milk and honey." There were rivers, lakes, and fertile soil. They would be able to grow anything they wanted. They even brought samples of the abundant fruit they found.

However, along with that great report, there were ten out of the twelve who were not so excited. They revealed their fear by stating that, "Yes, it is a beautiful land, for sure, but we have a serious problem. The cities have thick, high walls around them. The people are giants! We were like grasshoppers in their sight. We can never go in. They will overtake us, and we will be destroyed."

Caleb and Joshua were the only two spies who did not agree with the report of the ten. Appealing for the people to remember their history, they reminded them, "Of course, we can go in. The God who delivered us from Egypt, the God who opened the Red Sea, the God who has fed us every day in the wilderness can certainly take us home." But the majority took the side of the ten doubters, and they cried all night. They had seen the power of this God, and had been delivered by Him, but they still did not trust Him. Their faith was not strong enough yet.

In their frenzy of confusion, they became irrational and determined they would find another leader who would turn them around and take them back to the slavery of Egypt. They were too terrified to go into their promised land if they were just going to die when they crossed the border. They thought it would be better living their lives out as slaves rather than die at the hands of these giants. Like at the Red Sea, once again it was a time of total confusion, chaos and disorder.

The fickleness of the human heart was on full display. When things go well, God is wonderful. When it's not going so well, then the tendency to take matters into one's own hand becomes the typical response. It started with Eve when the enemy suggested God could not be trusted and has been the root of trouble and rebellion against God ever since. Of course, the enemy was pleased and satisfied with all the fear, disagreement and bedlam that must have taken over as a result of the distrust of God that they displayed.

Moses talked with God and begged to know what to do. He also begged God to forgive the people's doubt of Him and His ability to save them. God finally said He would forgive but added that He would turn them back into the wilderness, where they would remain a year for each day the spies had been gone. That meant that the entire multitude of people would wander aimlessly for forty long years. Everyone who was twenty years of age and older at that time would die during those forty years and be buried in the sand. It would be an entirely new generation of people who would finally enter the promised land they would be able to call home.

And so it was. For the next forty years they existed on water from the rock, and a daily serving of manna that God miraculously provided. When they awoke each morning, the manna was there on the ground like a powdery snow covering that they would gather for their families. It contained all the nutrients to keep them healthy. I wonder how one eats the same menu for forty years?

Their resources were the constant daily miracles coming from the hand of God. They were not able to provide anything on their own. God faithfully met their needs. Their clothes didn't wear out, their sandals stayed strong. They worshiped at the tent tabernacle. They moved from place to place, and they wandered around for four decades. How exhausting it all must have been. And, to top it all off, there were numerous funerals every day as the older generation passed away.

Tucked into the record of their hot, dusty existence, we find numerous complaints to Moses, who demonstrated his steadfast patience with their whining voices. At times, their frustration broke out into open rebellion. The highlights of their long, wearisome journey are recorded in the Biblical book of Numbers.

The good news is that forty years is not forever, and eventually it came to an end. This new generation of people once again found themselves back at the border, ready to move in and inhabit their homeland. There would be no one here older than sixty years of age except Moses, his brother Aaron, and the two trusting spies, Caleb and Joshua. Moses' sister Miriam, who had guarded him in the river basket, had passed away a few months earlier than this. How excited the people must have been that this long, grinding journey would finally come to an end.

The water from the rock that they had relied upon suddenly stopped flowing. Instead of taking that as a sign that God was ready to take them into a land where they would find all the water they would ever need, the people panicked. Once again, they ran to Moses, as they had done so many times, and complained to him. God had demonstrated to them that He was powerful, capable and was worthy of trust, but the people were still not free from their fear and inability to believe that God would see them through.

Moses is described as the meekest man who ever lived. However, on this day his meekness was set on the shelf for a consequential moment. The people's mistrust of God one more time was more than he could handle, causing his emotions to boil over. God asked Moses to go and calmly speak to the rock and God would once again provide water for them. It was actually a metaphor teaching us that God wants us to come and speak to Him (prayer) when we have a need. But Moses had had enough. He was angry, and for a brief moment ignored his filters.

He and Aaron stepped up to the rock before the people and Moses shouted at them, "You rebels. Must we bring water from this rock for you again?" And then instead of speaking to the rock as he had been instructed, he took his staff and struck the rock, two times. Water came gushing forth and the people were refreshed. However, God was not pleased with Moses for taking ownership of the miracle when he said, "Must WE bring water from this rock?" God sadly informed both Moses and Aaron that they who had been leading from the beginning would in fact not see the people safely into the promised homeland. It was devastating to Moses. He pleaded with God to change His mind, but God did not.

Before Moses died, we have a record of three different times when he addressed the people and gave heartfelt instruction for the days ahead. He continually reminded them of all that God had done for them. He pleaded with them to trust the God who had brought them through all the events of their history. He instructed them on what they must do in the land where they were going in order to honor God. Moses loved the people, encouraged them, and admonished them to be faithful, always. And then he said good-bye to them. After all he had been through with them, he was not able to watch them settle into their homes. It was a sad day for Moses and for the people. He climbed to the top of nearby Mount Nebo where God opened his eyes with a telescopic view of the land the Israelites were to inherit. He could clearly see all its borders and was given a glimpse into the future for the people he had loved so deeply. This was the place where his life ended.

The Book of Exodus tells the exciting story of the people being set free from slavery in Egypt, surviving the ten plagues and the opening of the Red Sea. It is here we also find the presentation of the Ten Commandments and the laws governing the nation of Israel, along with some of the early events in their journey toward the Promised Land.

The Book of Leviticus outlines all the guidelines and laws regarding the sacrifices and offerings the people were to bring to God. Leviticus also records the instruction on the celebration feasts they were to annually observe in their worship experiences before God.

The Book of Numbers records the wilderness wanderings of the people and some of the highlights of those long, weary forty years.

Moses' three sermons containing his faithful instructions to the people can be found in the Book of Deuteronomy.

GOD WANTS US TO REMEMBER:

- God's prophetic word can be counted on even if it takes hundreds of years to see the details actually play out.

- God demonstrated through the plagues, the Red Sea rescue, and the provision of water and manna to sustain His people in the desert that He is capable of anything we might ever need from Him. He loves it when we personalize that evidence and trust Him always.

- In the rescue of His people from slavery in Egypt, God demonstrated that His Holy attributes are above challenge. When the haughty Pharaoh asked who God was that he should honor Him, God answered His question with divine power, much to Pharaoh's and Egypt's detriment.

- God's Ten Commandments, or life principles, are only and always for our well-being. His desire is that we recognize these principles as His guidelines to keep us safe and fulfilled as we live in harmony with Him, and with each other.

- God is only loving in all that He does. When He turned the people back into the wilderness, His purpose was to continue to teach them that He was a God they could rely on since they had not demonstrated that they trusted Him just yet. We do well when we trust Him quickly, based on the evidence we have from the stories we read, and the personal experiences we have gone through in our own lives.

- God may seem harsh when He would not let Aaron and Moses lead the people into the Promised Land. He was reminding us that He will never just turn His back on, or just "wink" at rebellion and disobedience. There was a reason He asked Moses to speak to the rock which will be revealed later in this book. He will always forgive us for rebellion when we ask, but more than that He wants to deliver us from it. A submissive heart is the best gift we can offer the God of the universe.

Don't be afraid. Just stand still and watch the LORD rescue you. The Egyptians you see today will never be seen again. The LORD himself will fight for you.

EXODUS 14:13-15

Moses spent forty years thinking he was somebody, forty years learning he was nobody, and forty years discovering what God can do with a nobody.

D. L. MOODY

I will be with you as I was with Moses. I will not fail you or abandon you.

JOSHUA 1:5

7

HOME AT LAST

Finally, after decades of delay, the people were once again on the doorstep of their new home. The journey from Egypt to Canaan should have taken a few short weeks at most but instead had taken forty long years.

Moses had died, just before the journey ended. In their grief the people realized that a new leader would be needed to finish the journey and take them over the Jordan River into the Promised Land.

Joshua was chosen, one of the two faithful spies from this same place forty years earlier. His faith in God prepared him for the task ahead of him. The book of Joshua chronicles his life and work as the next leader of the Israelite people. His biography records the tumultuous years in which the people worked to conquer the territory. He then guided them as they spread out, claimed, and settled their families throughout the land.

Like bookends, just as God had opened the Red Sea to allow the people to finally gain their freedom from Egypt, He now performed a similar miracle as they entered their homeland. The people were on the east side of the Jordan River and needed to cross it to complete their journey.

God asked the priests to walk down into the river carrying the Ark of the Covenant, one of the holy articles of worship that was part of their Sanctuary services. As they stepped into the water, the river suddenly parted. The water in the river upstream stopped as if a dam had suddenly been constructed, and the water downstream flowed away to the Dead Sea. The people crossed over on dry ground, to finally walk on the land they could claim as theirs. They were home! Caleb and Joshua were the only two who were older than twenty years of age at the time they left Egypt. Those who stood here now could barely remember life in Egypt and the Red Sea rescue. Most of them only knew the history from hearing the stories they had been told.

The challenge ahead of them all was that the land was already occupied with cities, groups, families, small nations and armies of people who had been living there ever since the time of Abraham.

The book of Joshua is the story of wars and conquest. God had promised this territory to the ancestors of Abraham, and the time had now come to claim it. The people who presently occupied the land were familiar with the amazing things being told about what the God of the Hebrew nation had done for His people, and they were terrified because of what they were hearing. They had heard of the plagues in Egypt. They had heard about the walk through the Red Sea, the parting of the Jordan River, as well as the size of this nation of people who were now inside their borders. They were heartsick. They wanted nothing to do with these people or their God.

One of the most famous stories is the very first battle the Israelites engaged in. They were instructed by God to simply march around the city of Jericho, then go back to camp. The people of Jericho were completely confused by what they saw. They were ready for battle, feeling safe inside their thick-walled city, but this enemy army just marched around it, and then went home. The next day, they did it again. Each day they did the exact same thing. The people inside the walls could make no sense of this strange war strategy, and they had no idea how to engage with this army. The mystery of these strange events no doubt had people talking non-stop at the local Starbucks, around water coolers, and late into the night on their back decks.

On day seven, the Israelite army once again walked around the city, but instead of going home, when they finished circling the city they walked around it again. Then again. And again, for a total of seven times. When they had finished the seventh trip around the walls, everyone stopped, turned and faced the city. The priests blew their trumpets, and the soldiers all shouted a war cry. As they did so, the city walls simply collapsed and tumbled down before their very eyes. Then the army quickly rushed in and conquered the city.

How quickly the news must have spread about that event, only adding an increased level of foreboding terror to what the people of the land already felt.

At another time, Joshua and his army were engaged in battle and the sun was about to go down. They were not finished, the battle was not yet over, and darkness was about to interfere with the outcome. Joshua spoke to the sun and commanded it to stand still. To everyone's amazement, the sun stopped its movement toward sunset. The sun stayed in the sky without going down for about a whole day. When the battle was won, the sun continued its natural descent into the western horizon.

It was obvious that God was present with His people, and supernatural events attested to His work on their behalf. Just as He had rescued them from Egypt, He was now finishing the task for them. In just a few short years, the entire land had been conquered, and it was time to settle and rest. As the people followed the leadings of the LORD, they continued to make their way through the land. As battles were won, with the resulting territories taken, the people settled their families, tribe by tribe. In the area that is still known as Israel today, the children of Abraham, Isaac and Jacob finally began to experience the peace they had not known for over four hundred years.

The conquest of and settling down into the land of Canaan is recorded in the Book of Joshua. The first half of the book is about the wars they engaged in; the last half is a record of how the people finally put down roots and began to enjoy the benefits of being home. It was time to experience the life of God's blessing that He had desired for them.

Ever since their deliverance from Egypt, God had been inviting His people into a close, trusting relationship with Him. The trusting and the blessings would go hand in hand. The blessings would be poured out in abundance as the people trusted God, worshiping Him, and following His leading. It was not meant to be a reward for trusting as much as it was to be the display of the ongoing, vibrant relationship God desired for and with His people.

Tragically, as years went by, the people moved away from their worship of God. The gods of the people of Canaan became attractive to them, and they decided to replace the worship of their living God with the worship of wooden and stone idols.

This worship often descended into spiritual rituals that were nothing more than emotional, sensual behaviors and activities, even including public prostitution, which was explained away as an offering to a god or goddess of love. Some even went so far as to sacrifice their own children, all in the name of religion. This tragic and horrifying "worship" was nothing at all that the living God desired or expected from them.

Hebrew life slowly evolved into predictable spiritual cycles. They would drift away from their relationship with God, then be reminded of the futility of seeking guidance from a man-made idol of wood. They would soon find themselves in hard circumstances, usually from an invading army, then turn back and cry out to God once again.

God's sadness at the futility of it all is summarized in a quote from the book of Judges. "This is what the LORD, the God of Israel, says: I brought you up out of slavery in Egypt. I rescued you from the Egyptians and from all who oppressed you. I drove out your enemies and gave you their land. I told you, 'I am the LORD your God. You must not worship the gods of the Amorites in whose land you now live.' But you have not listened to me." Judges 6:9,10.

Do you hear the heart cry of God here, expressing His emotion because His chosen people repeatedly turned their backs on Him? We continually see the patience and perseverance of God as He worked to rescue them and bring them back to Him, time after time. The enemy paints God as a harsh dictator and too many have believed that lie.

With each new challenging situation, God would often call specific people to respond to the next crisis. These Judges, as they were called, often led the nation into battle with surrounding nations, trusting in God for deliverance from their enemies. The record of the nation's continual teeter-totter experience in their relationship to God is painful to read about.

While there were twelve judges mentioned in the history of Israel, one of the most famous of the Judges was a man named Samson. He was best known for his brute physical strength, and the amazing feats he could accomplish in the battles against the invading Philistine army sound like modern day Superpower Heroes.

He killed a lion with his bare hands. He singlehandedly killed one thousand enemies in one day. One time they thought they had finally trapped Samson in the city of Gaza, (yes the same Gaza we hear about in the news today) when they closed and locked the city gates with him inside. No problem! He simply picked up the gates along with ripping out the gate posts that anchored them to the ground, carried them all away and left them piled in a heap on the top of a hill nearby.

Samson's tragic life is bittersweet. He was blessed by God and his hair was a token of that trust relationship. He was to never cut it. However, a woman named Delilah, who pretended to love him, kept pleading with him to tell her what the secret of his great strength was. He played with answers for her but finally gave in and told her that if his hair was cut, he would be no stronger than anyone else.

She tested his secret out that very night by cutting his hair while he slept. Sure enough, when his enemies came to him the next day, he was easily defeated and taken prisoner. After putting out his eyes, they made him work the treadmill, grinding grain like an ox. Day after weary day, as he endlessly walked in circles, his connection with God was re-established and his hair grew back. He may have been blind but his heart found its way home.

The Philistine people were having a celebration and in their drunken state called for Samson to be brought from prison so they could make fun of him. Samson was led to the center of the temple where three thousand people were gathered inside and on the roof. He asked the young man leading him to put his hands on the center pillars so he could lean and rest. As he did so, he prayed a repentant prayer to God and asked for strength, which he received. By leaning on the pillars he pushed them over and destroyed the whole building. All the people in it died, including himself. It was his final act of victory against the enemies of Israel.

Samson's biography is like a short summary of the entire nation's relationship with God. When they trusted and served Him, they were a strong and united nation. When they forgot Him, and did what was right in their own eyes, they were weak, disoriented and lost. We read about a series of seven different cycles which continued for a period of approximately four hundred years. The last sentence in the book of Judges describes the whole time period by telling us that rather than collectively seeking God as a nation, "all the people did whatever seemed right in their own eyes." Judges 21:25. This is the condition of any human heart that is disconnected from God.

Beginning with Adam and Eve, the anthem of going alone, independently, outside of God's plan, is played out repeatedly. Both through the lives of individuals and displayed through the history of the nation as a whole, we are reminded that when people place their trust in God, their lives find purpose and the blessing of His presence. When He is ignored, He is a gentleman and does not force His way, but He lets people painfully discover the results of living a life without Him.

Sadly however, God's chosen people, the family He had chosen to provide the ultimate blessing to all the people on Earth, were about to take their rejection of Him and His leading to a whole new level.

The Book of Joshua relates the story of the history of Israel through the years of conquering and resettling in their Promised Land.

The story of the tumultuous four hundred years of the Judges can be found in the Book of Judges.

GOD WANTS US TO REMEMBER:

- He continues to fulfill His word. He promised Abraham that after much time in slavery his family would come back to the land He had given to them when He first called Abraham to leave his home in Ur. The promise finally came true.

- This is the family through whom "All the nations of the earth would be blessed." God is looking after them and continues to guide their journey. When they turned their back on Him and began to worship the gods of the nations around them, He would continue to call them back to relationship with Him. He is relentless in His pursuit of all His people, including you and me.

- When people or nations decide to "do what is right in their own eyes" and ignore the presence and leading of God, the consequences are often tough. The lessons learned as we find our way back to Him are invaluable, as long as we pay attention to them and apply them appropriately.

Study this Book of instruction continually. Meditate on it day and night so you will be sure to obey everything written in it. Only then will you prosper and succeed in all you do.

JOSHUA 1:8

Would you prefer the gods your ancestors served, or will it be the gods of the Amorites in whose land you now live? But as for me and my family, we will serve the Lord.

JOSHUA 24:15

8

KINGS AND PROPHETS

Human nature has a habit of comparing. We like what we see in the character of others, and we want that. We compare our car to other cars, and often, we like those better. We compare many things. Houses, clothing, bank accounts and appearance, often tending to like what we see "over there" more than what we have "over here". The enemy tempted Eve with, "If you eat this fruit, you will be like God." She wanted "that," and went ahead and ate the fruit. That's how it all started.

The last judge in Israel was a man named Samuel, who was also respected and accepted as a spiritual leader, even referred to as a prophet. However, his sons did not hold his values and were known to be men who took bribes, not afraid to skew justice in favor of themselves or their friends. The people were afraid that Samuel's sons would have no boundaries after Samuel died.

The Israelites had noticed that other nations had kings to rule over them. These kings would always be ready to move into battle and were present to provide constant leadership. There was no gap between leaders, there would always be a king. The people compared themselves to what the other nations were doing and wanted what "they" had.

The people went to Samuel and said, "You are getting old. We don't like the activities of your sons, and we want you to find us a king, like all the other nations."

This was a gut-kick to Samuel! He loved that God was their King and that while God chose the Judges to guide the people, He was still the ultimate ruler of the people. If they chose a king, they would be taking leadership away from God and placing it in the hands of one man.

Samuel talked to God and relayed their request. God simply said, "Let them have their way. They are not rejecting you, they are rejecting Me. They have been rejecting Me ever since I brought them out of Egypt. They are now rejecting you, too. Warn them about what they are doing and then let them choose."

The ultimate gift of love that God gives to all mankind is the free will to make any decision we want to make. Just as God had given Adam and Eve the freedom to choose to eat the fruit or not, He still to this day honors people's right to make their own choices. What He also wants us to know is that along with that choice we also choose the consequences that accompany them. They could make their choice to have a king, but they would also reap the result of that choice.

Samuel went to the people and said, "If you choose a king, here is what you can expect. This king will call your sons to provide services for him. He will call your sons to cultivate his fields. Some will be called to make weapons of war. They will be pressed into battle at his request. He will take your daughters to serve in his courts. He will take your fields, your vineyards. He will take a portion of your crops and herds in taxes. You will be his servants. And you will cry out in those days, but you have made your own choice."

They ignored his advice and simply said, "We want a king over us, like all the other nations." God, being the gentleman that He is, let them have their way, knowing they were going to regret their decision. He told Samuel to find them a king.

KING SAUL

The first king of Israel was a man named Saul. He was shy, actually so afraid to take the role that he hid himself. When they brought him out of hiding, they could not help but notice that he was tall and handsome. These features were the convincing factors for them. They did not know a lot about him, but the outward appearance looked good, so they declared him the king.

Are we not just like them? I remember as a boy cheering for the hockey team whose goalie had the nicest, newest looking goalie pads. How many people today have voted for a politician because they liked his/her hair, or his/her good looks? Marriages have broken up when people realize that the beauty or features they were attracted to was all on the outside, but character qualities that were missing on the inside made it impossible to have a healthy relationship with that same person. The method they used to choose Saul as king demonstrates that this approach is not new.

Samuel again warned them, saying, "You have rejected your God by this decision," but they insisted on making Saul their king.

Saul reigned over the nation for approximately forty years. During that time, he demonstrated continual selfish and self-serving behavior. He was known to be impulsive and moody, never recognized as a spiritual leader. During the decades that he ruled he did not make worship of the Creator God a priority. He led the people in a series of battles and was known as a man of war, but he also displayed a fearful sense of cowardice as well.

Some twenty-five years after Saul had become king, Samuel gave him specific instructions from God that he was expected to follow in every detail. Saul only partially obeyed the command and found logical reasons why he should do it his way. He was defensive for his own wisdom in the matter and put up an argument in order to justify himself. The result was that God told Samuel He had in fact rejected Saul as king. From then on, Saul was king in name only but would no longer receive the blessing of God.

God then sent Samuel on a mission to Bethlehem to visit a man named Jesse, who was the father of eight sons. They were to worship together and then enjoy a meal. God told Samuel that He would indicate to him which son would be God's choice to be the next king of Israel, and Samuel would anoint that one. Samuel asked to see all of Jesse's sons.

The first one stood before him, and Samuel was sure that he would be the one. He was tall and impressive to Samuel. God spoke to him with a message that is good for all of us to remember when it comes to judging the character of people. He said, "Don't judge him by his appearance or height, for I have rejected him. The LORD doesn't see things the way you see them. People judge by outward appearance, but the LORD looks at the heart." 1 Samuel 16:7

The next son stood before Samuel, and then the next, and so on through all seven young men who were present, but God never indicated that there was one that he should pick. Samuel asked if Jesse had any other sons, and he was informed that yes, the youngest was out in the fields tending his father's sheep. "Send for him at once," said Samuel.

That son, David, was brought to him and the LORD said to Samuel, "This is the one, anoint him." From that moment on, David received a special blessing of the powerful presence of the Spirit of God in his life. David went back to being a shepherd, always remembering that he had in fact been chosen to be king one day. God has a way of surprising us with His choices.

Saul was still king and around the same time that David was anointed, the nation of Israel was at war again with a people known as the Philistines. For a time during this conflict, the two armies were encamped, facing each other on either side of a valley. Each day, a giant Philistine soldier named Goliath would come out and call out, challenging the army of Israel to send a warrior to fight a one-on-one battle with him. He promised that the winner of that event would determine the outcome of the war. "If your man is able to kill me, then we will be your slaves. But if I kill him, you will be our slaves. I defy the armies of Israel. Send me a man who will fight with me!" 1 Samuel 17:9,10

Goliath was simply a bully using his size and voice to intimidate Israel's army. So far it had been working.

One day David went to the camp to take food for his brothers who were soldiers in Saul's army, arriving about the time Goliath made his boastful speech for the day. David was personally insulted that this giant could speak so arrogantly against the armies of the living God and wanted to know why this man was not challenged. Because David voiced his conviction on the matter out loud, he was taken to meet King Saul, face to face.

Saul looked at him and said, "You are too young and inexperienced to fight a man like this." David responded, "I look after my father's sheep. I have killed bears and lions who came to attack the sheep. This Philistine will be like one of them for he has defied the armies of the living God." David's faith was limitless, and his confidence was not able to be ignored. As the king and leader of Israel, Saul should have been the one to demonstrate that faith in God and go face this Philistine giant himself, but boldness was not in Saul's nature. He offered David his own battle armor and equipment, but after trying it on David took it off again because it didn't fit him and just did not feel right.

The two armies waited and watched until suddenly, out of the crowd on Israel's side of the valley, David appeared, walking toward Goliath. He had no weapons, nor any shield for war. All he had was a sling for throwing rocks, which he had mastered during the countless hours he spent with his father's sheep. After stopping at the brook to pick up five stones and putting them in his shepherd's pouch, he then moved forward to face this haughty enemy head on. Boy with faith in God VS giant man with faith in himself!

The Philistine giant became incensed at the insult of having this "child" be chosen to fight him. In anger and screaming with rage, he pushed back the helmet on his head, providing just the target David needed. With the precision of a sniper, David unleashed a rock from the power of that sling and drove it right into the forehead of Goliath, who crashed down like a mighty redwood tree. David quickly killed Goliath with the very sword Goliath had threatened David with only moments before. Panic set in, and instead of bowing as servants as the proposal had been presented, the Philistines ran like scared children. The battle was over, and David was the hero.

One can only imagine the news and gossip that spread through the nation about David. In the weeks and years that followed, Saul became a jealous, insecure, weak little man in the face of David's popularity. During the remainder of Saul's life, he spent much of it in hot pursuit of David, determined to kill him. However, David was the LORD's anointed next king of Israel, and along with a band of renegade soldiers who assembled with him, David avoided all opportunity for Saul to carry out his vengeance.

On two occasions, David was in a position where he could have easily killed Saul, but David respected the fact that Saul was still the chosen king. He knew he had been anointed king and was submissive to God's timing as to when he should occupy the throne so was not willing to take matters to destroy Saul into his own hands. One time, David and his men were hiding deep in the recesses of a cave, and in the light of the entrance he saw Saul come into that very same cave. David crept forward in the darkness and cut off a piece of his robe. When Saul left the cave, David followed him out into the sunlight, called to him and showed him the piece of the garment that he had cut, proving that he could have easily killed him. Saul was humbled at the truth of what David had done and assured David he could live in peace.

That didn't last long. Saul's jealousy returned, and he set out to kill David once again. One night David found Saul's camp with sleeping soldiers all around the slumbering king. David crept in and took Saul's spear and water container that were lying beside him, then quietly slipped away. From a safe distance he called to wake Saul up. Holding up the items he had taken, he taunted the soldiers guarding Saul, proving to them that they had failed to keep him safe. The only reason

Saul was alive was because David had chosen not to kill him. Once again, David proved he was no threat to Saul. The character of each man was fully on display.

King Saul eventually died in a battle with the Philistine army, the same nation they had been fighting when they met the giant, Goliath. Saul was struck and immobilized. Realizing he could not survive, he asked his servant to put him to death so that his enemy would not have the pleasure, but the servant refused. Saul then committed suicide by intentionally falling on his own sword. It was a tragic end to the man who had been crowned as the first king of God's chosen people.

KING DAVID

When David heard the news of Saul's death, he wept and mourned for Saul and did not eat for a whole day. Even though Saul had made David's life miserable for so many years, and that he himself had been anointed king some fifteen years earlier, he was in grief over the news that the king of his nation had died. This is the heart of a leader. He wasn't thinking of himself, he was sad for the life of a man who turned out to be such a disappointment.

David's life demonstrated that his character and spiritual guidance of his people toward worship of the Creator God was exactly opposite to that of Saul. David went on to become revered as the greatest king the nation of Israel ever had. His courage and strength came about because of his strong faith and trust in God. He had the soft heart of a shepherd, and he had the strong heart of a battle warrior. He was a man of worship, known as "The sweet singer of Israel." He is the author of approximately half of the psalms in the Book of Psalms, which are simply hymns and songs that would have been set to music and sung in praise to God. The most famous is Psalm 23. I quote it here from the New King James Version of the Bible.

The Lord is my shepherd;
I shall not want.
He makes me to lie down in green pastures;
He leads me beside the still waters
He restores my soul;
He leads me in the paths of righteousness.
For His name's sake.
Yea, though I walk through the valley of the shadow of death,
I will fear no evil;
For You are with me; Your rod and Your staff, they comfort me.
You prepare a table before me in the presence of my enemies;
You anoint my head with oil;
My cup runs over.
Surely goodness and mercy shall follow me
All the days of my life;
And I will dwell in the house of the LORD forever.

As mighty as king David was, he also had a dark chapter in his life, a spectacular failure. One day, while on the roof of his palace, he noticed a woman bathing on the roof of her house nearby. The rooftops were flat, so people often carried out some of their daily activities there. The power of temptation overcame him, and he sent for her. Since he was king, no matter how she might have felt, she did not know how to refuse when she was told the king wanted to see her. Her name was Bathsheba, a married woman, whose husband, Uriah, was away at war.

When we play with fire, sometimes it burns. When she discovered that she was pregnant, she sent word to David that she was carrying his child. He panicked and invited Uriah home from battle for a visit. After being updated on the state of the battle, David sent Uriah home to Bathsheba, hoping he would spend time with his wife and thus conceal the truth of her child. Uriah refused to go home and slept in the accommodations provided for the palace guard. David was shocked and asked him why. He said, "The men in the army are out on the battlefield and not able to enjoy the pleasure of the company of their wives. How could I do such a thing?" David kept him in Jerusalem for three days, even inviting him to dinner and getting him drunk, but Uriah slept at the palace gate again even though his wife was close by. Here was a man who displayed the integrity that David had failed to demonstrate.

In desperation, David went to plan B. He sent a message back to the army commander with Uriah himself. The instruction to the commander was that he was to put Uriah at the front of the battle and then withdraw from him, leaving him unprotected. The expected result took place and Uriah died that day. David's sin was safe, or so he thought.

Everything came to light when God revealed the facts to a prophet named Nathan, who paid David a visit and confronted him about the matter. As sad as the story is, David stepped up and accepted total accountability for the situation when he was faced with the truth. So many would avoid acknowledgement of any wrongdoing, maybe even going so far as to blame Bathsheba herself for bathing outside in the first place. David did not deny his part and was totally accountable for what he had done. His confession is probably the clearest plea for forgiveness the Bible ever records. It begins like this, but you may want to read it in its entirety:

Have mercy on me, O God, because of your unfailing love.
Because of your great compassion, blot out the stains of my guilt.
Purify me from my sin.
For I recognize my rebellion; it haunts me day and night.
Against you, and you alone, have I sinned;
I have done what is evil in your sight. Psalm 51:1-4

David is known for his strong and mighty leadership, and for his demonstration of humility and repentance. Even with the guilt of arranging the death of Uriah on his hands to cover up his own sin of adultery with Uriah's wife, he was later described as a "man after God's own heart." Whenever Israel looks to find the pinnacle of their success as a nation, they point to the time of King David. This truly demonstrates that God is a God of mercy and forgiveness for anyone who humbly seeks Him, regardless of their past.

KING SOLOMON

Eventually Bathsheba did become David's wife. They later had a son and named him Solomon. David appointed Solomon to take his place on the throne after his death. Saul, David and Solomon each reigned as king for approximately forty years.

During the time that Solomon was king, a most exotic temple was built in Israel and dedicated to the worship of God. The people of Israel had been given instructions on how to build a temporary, tent-like sanctuary hundreds of years earlier, while they were wandering in the wilderness. Now, for the first time, they had a permanent house of worship where they could come to present their sacrifices. This building was a place of wonder and awe for any person traveling to Jerusalem.

When he became king, Solomon asked God for an extra measure of wisdom for the task ahead of him. God was pleased with the request and honored him with that gift. One example is demonstrated by how he managed a dilemma between two ladies who were brought to him with a very personal but serious conflict.

The women were friends who lived together, and both had babies at around the same time. One of the mothers unfortunately rolled on her baby in the night, and the baby died. She quietly swapped the two babies and claimed that the live baby was hers. The other mother was heartbroken and was absolutely and adamantly sure that her baby was the one who was still alive. They argued back and forth in a "she said, she said" scenario in front of Solomon, who of course would not know for sure which one was telling the truth.

If ever there was a time that called for wisdom, this was it. After listening carefully to hear both ladies, Solomon simply said, "Bring a sword and we will cut the live baby in two, and each of you can have half." The mother of the live baby cried out, begging him not to do that. "Let the baby live! The other mother can have it." The other mother agreed with the plan and said to go ahead and divide the child. Solomon immediately knew from their responses that it would be the true mother who would rather have the baby alive than to have it killed for no reason. He sent her home with her child.

The book of Proverbs in the Bible is a record of many wise sayings and teachings, the majority of which are attributed to Solomon. Much of Solomon's wisdom is recorded there, including many good life skills still applicable today. Such as:

Choose a good reputation over great riches; being held in high esteem is better than silver or gold. Proverbs 22:1

Love prospers when a fault is forgiven, but dwelling on it separates friends. Proverbs 17:9

However, Solomon also had a weakness. The Bible states that Solomon had seven hundred wives, and three hundred concubines. Yes, you read that correctly. Concubines were women of his harem, not married to him, but were to be available to him for companionship and pleasure at his request.

Ladies, how would you like to receive a greeting card from Solomon, your husband, reminding you how important you were to him out of all thousand of his wives or companions?

Solomon wrote the book, Song of Solomon, where in poetic form he speaks of romantic relationships, something that he would have knowledge about for sure. Toward the end of his life, Solomon wrote the book of Ecclesiastes (Ee-cleez-ee-ast-ease), where he acknowledged the futile search for meaning that he had spent his life pursuing in all the wrong places. He summed it up by stating it was all "Vanity!"

If we were to summarize the spiritual leadership of the first three kings of Israel, we would say that Saul was a man who didn't give God any significant part or perspective as he lived his life. He was not a follower of God.

David was the opposite to Saul and was a man after God's heart. It would be accurate to say that David was totally committed to seek God for guidance as he served his time as king. In spite of his failure, he is an example of what God loves to do for people who humbly repent for past regrets and mistakes. David's whole heart was dedicated to seeking God and worshipping Him.

Solomon started strong, seeking God for wisdom, but then allowed temptation of riches and years of pleasure to occupy his mind and time. In the later years of his life, he realized the vanity of his seeking for meaning in places where God could not be found. Solomon had a divided heart when it came to allowing God to influence his leadership skills.

A DIVIDED NATION

Saul, David and Solomon are the only three kings who reigned over the united nation of all twelve tribes of Israel. In approximately 930 B.C., because of political events that took place shortly after the death of Solomon, the nation was divided into two parts. Ten of the tribes in the Northern part of the country formed a nation, retaining the name Israel. The other two tribes, the descendants of Jacob's sons Judah and Benjamin, set up their own kingdom in the Southern part of the land and named that nation Judah.

From then on each nation had their own king, and their own capital city. The capital of Israel was Samaria. Jerusalem remained the capital city of the nation of Judah.

In the centuries of history that follow, we find a pitiful account of the succession of kings in both nations who had completely lost the vision of God's purpose for His chosen people. During the history of the Northern tribes of Israel, there were nineteen kings who took their turn on the throne. The Southern kingdom of Judah lasted a few years longer than Israel and had twenty different kings to lead them during the history of their tumultuous years.

Out of all thirty-nine kings combined, only eight were leaders who desired to lead the nation back to God. These eight were all kings of the Southern kingdom of Judah. That means there was never a king to sit on the throne of the ten Northern tribes who had the desire to lead the people to be a spiritual nation, or to seek His guidance during their time as ruler.

No doubt there were always some individuals who loved and sincerely served God the best way they knew how, but as a nation they were never led as a collective body to make God the center of their worship or their politics. What a sad chapter in the life of the people God had chosen for the purpose of being a blessing to all the nations of the earth. Not only would a savior come through them, but they were also to be a people who would model the blessings and honor of faithfully serving a loving Creator God.

PROPHETS

Despite experiencing the pain of being rejected as He was, God couldn't simply stand by and let His people just walk away without at least appealing to them. God is not a god of force who would bully his people into loving Him. He was a God who never stopped loving His people and was always ready to quickly welcome them should they turn back to Him.

At numerous times, God called certain people, known as prophets, to communicate a variety of appeals and warnings to the people He loved. He would give the prophets messages to share, calling the nations back to Him where He could once again bless them in the ways He had always intended to. He often allowed them to suffer the consequences of their rebellion against Him, but He was never far away and continued to remind them that He was there and wanted to fill their land with unlimited blessings.

The entire historical saga contained in the Old Testament is told within the first seventeen books, from Genesis to Esther. The other twenty-two books of the Old Testament were written within the timeline contained in the historical books. Of those, five were either books of Psalms (songs), poetry, or philosophical in nature.

The seventeen remaining books are prophetic in nature, five referred to as major prophets, and twelve considered minor prophets. (No, that does not mean that the minor prophets were all under eighteen years of age!) The distinction between major and minor prophets is entirely based on the length of the writings that came from each of them. All were authentic messages from God to the people, some just longer and more detailed than others.

The prophets did not choose themselves to take on the role, nor did any one of them apply for the job. Each one felt a calling on his life and believed it was his duty to share with the people what he had been commissioned to present, even if it was unpopular. The prophets would receive their messages through dreams or visions, or sometimes simple messages of conviction that would come to them which they felt compelled to write out or preach. They did not want to risk being disobedient to God and fail to relay the message they believed He had compelled them with. The calling of a prophet was sacred, serious, and anything but easy. They were scoffed at, tortured, even put to death for their convictions and the messages they conveyed.

When confronted with a message from God's prophet, the first question for the people of Israel should have been, "What if it's true?" Should they ignore it or take it as a loving invitation, leading them back to a restored relationship with Him?

The record of Samuel and the life of King Saul is found in the Book of First Samuel.

The last years of Samuel and the life of King David is found in the Book of Second Samuel.

The Book of First Kings tells us what we know of King Solomon.

The Book of Second Kings is an account of the divided kingdoms of Israel and Judah.

The Book of First Chronicles is a record of the life of David from a different author.

The Book of Second Chronicles provides a history of the Southern Kingdom of Judah.

GOD WANTS US TO REMEMBER:

- Because God loves His people with a never-ending love, He allows them to make damaging decisions should they choose to do so, even if those decisions will not ever serve them as well as if they followed His leadings in the first place. However, He is always there beside them to bring back their blessings when they choose to turn back to Him.

- When the wisdom of God is followed and allowed to have influence in the life of an individual or nation, the results are always full of blessings. We notice that when the governing king would turn the people back to God, good things always happened for them, but sadly only eight times.

- God never lets His people go too far without calling and warning them. He was quick to send His prophets on a mission with the difficult task of sharing the messages from God to His rebellious people. He could not bear to see them turn their backs on Him without at least letting them know that they mattered to Him.

You are free to make choices. You are not free to escape the consequences of those choices.

HOWARD HENDRICKS

Happiness is not a reward — it is a consequence. Suffering is not a punishment — it is a result.

ROBERT GREEN INGERSOLL

It only takes a second to make a choice. Yet the choice made in that second can have ramifications for a lifetime.

ANONYMOUS

9

CHOICES HAVE CONSEQUENCES

The Kings of the divided realms were mostly bent on serving any god but the living God. For hundreds of years, God sent His prophets to warn and appeal to His people.

Because the messages went unheeded, and because most of the kings had no desire or will to lead a spiritual revival toward God, He finally allowed each nation to reap the consequences of their choices. Ultimately, when nations came to war with them, God was not there to protect them or bring them victory. They suffered defeat and loss as a result of leaving God out of their thoughts, plans and guidance.

The ten tribes of Israel in the North were overrun and completely dispersed by the neighboring nation of Assyria. Their captivity took place in the area we would know today as Northern Iraq and Syria, and their nation was no more. They are often referred to as the Ten Lost Tribes of Israel.

The two tribes of Judah survived for a hundred years longer than Israel due to the influence the eight God-fearing kings had on the nation. However, eventually Judah also suffered captivity at the hands of the nation of Babylon, under king Nebuchadnezzar (Neb-you-kad-nez-are). A large number of the people were exiled from Judah to Babylon, located in the area we would know today as Southern Iraq. Babylon then continued to control the land of Judah as a satellite province.

The Book of Daniel is the record of a young man, one of those exiled into captivity at that time. The experiences of Daniel and his friends, demonstrate the blessings of God in the life of those dedicated to obedience and an uncompromising personal relationship with Him. The book is a fascinating mixture of history, prophecy and personal stories.

We read how three of Daniel's friends were thrown into a burning fiery furnace because they would not worship a golden statue that King Nebuchadnezzar had created in his own honor. They miraculously survived and were seen walking around in the fire accompanied by a fourth person believed to have been God the Son.

Daniel himself was thrown into a lion's den because he would not stop praying to the Creator God, even when it had been decreed that no one could pray to anyone but the king for a period of thirty days. In the morning, he was untouched because, as he explained it, "an angel came and shut the lions' mouths."

One night, Nebuchadnezzar had a dream that he was sure had significant meaning, but he just could not remember what it was. The wise men of the kingdom were threatened with death if they would not be able to tell the king his dream, and its meaning. As was his habit, Daniel prayed about it. God showed him the dream and explained its prophetic significance. Daniel then told the king exactly what he had dreamed and explained that it was the God of Heaven who had revealed it to him. The king immediately recognized the details of the dream as Daniel explained it and was anxious to find out its meaning.

Daniel reminded him that he had seen a large statue made up of different types of metal. The head was gold, the arms were silver, the belly was brass, and the legs were iron. The feet were a mixture of iron and clay. Then a stone, cut out without hands, came from a nearby mountain and struck the image on the feet, grinding the image up into powder after which it was all blown away like dust in the wind. Then the stone expanded and filled the whole earth. If I woke up after a dream like that, I would think there must be something significant about it too.

Daniel explained the meaning of the dream and said that King Nebuchadnezzar and Babylon were illustrated by the head of gold. Then, just like silver is inferior to gold, another nation, not as strong as Babylon, would overthrow and conquer them. Then a third, and finally a fourth kingdom would each take a turn to rule the world. Finally, the rock that ground up the image depicted that all the historical nations would be overcome by a supernatural kingdom that would grow to fill the whole earth.

History bears the facts that Medo-Persia was a weaker nation but was able to conquer Babylon. Greece then conquered Medo-Persia, and Rome conquered Greece. Each nation was on the world stage for hundreds of years before being replaced by the next one. Rome was not defeated by another nation but faded away as it disintegrated from within into ten small nations, thus the feet of iron and clay, materials that do not adhere to each other.

Eventually, the rock that arrives to grind it all up and blow it away represents the kingdom of God that will one day put an end to all nations as we know them today. God's kingdom will fill the whole earth, which is symbolic language for the prediction that it will never end.

The dream/prophecy accomplishes at least two things. It presented a birds-eye view of how the history of the world would unfold and closed with a promise that God will one day bring the world to an end. This all adds credibility to the Bible in that this basic prophecy unfolded with precise accuracy even though it was predicted hundreds of years before the events took place.

Daniel also received prophetic visions about some of the details and the timing of the coming savior of the world.

We never hear of the ten tribes of Israel returning to their homes. However, after seventy years in captivity, the nation of Judah was allowed the freedom to return to their homeland, and their capital city,

Jerusalem. The nation of Medo-Persia had conquered Babylon by that time, and it was under this new world power that they were allowed to experience a fresh start back in the land promised to them centuries earlier through Abraham.

The people returned in three stages.

In the Book of Ezra, we read about two separate events when masses of people returned to Judah. A man named Zerubbabel (Zer-uh-bah-bell) led a group of people back to restore the temple King Solomon had built, which had been destroyed when the nation of Judah was taken captive.

Then later, a man named Ezra led a group of people back to Jerusalem and taught them the law of God from the writings of Moses which had been forsaken for so many centuries.

In the book of Nehemiah we read of a third and last group of people to return, led by the man the book is named after. His work was to rebuild the wall that surrounded Jerusalem, which had also been destroyed along with the temple when Nebuchadnezzar conquered them. Due to the dedication and the excitement to bring the city back to life, the wall was completely rebuilt in just fifty-two days.

Between the first and second groups of people who returned, we find the story of Queen Esther as told in the book bearing her name. Esther was a Hebrew girl chosen to be the replacement for the queen of Persia, who had fallen out of favor with King Xerxes. (Zerk-sees)

Haman, a high-ranking official in the court of the king, encouraged King Xerxes to put out a decree that on a given day all the Hebrew people still living in the land would be put to death. Xerxes issued the decree not realizing that Esther herself was in danger. Realizing the peril that her people were in, Esther determined she would go to the king, identify her relationship to the condemned people and plead for their safety.

It was a law of the Persian nation that no one was to enter in to see the king without an invitation. When informed that Esther was there to meet with him, she could be accepted and invited into the king's presence and all would be well. Or if not, she could be executed.

Her bravery is a demonstration of amazing courage. She said, "though it is against the law, I will go in to see the king. If I must die, I must die." (Esther 4:16) Thankfully, Esther was accepted by the king at which time she invited him to a banquet she would prepare for him, as well as for Haman. As they dined, she invited them back to a second banquet the following day. While eating together this time, with Haman present, she unveiled Haman's plot to destroy her people. In a complete turn of events, Haman was instead executed and the Hebrew people were saved. By using her voice at the right time, God used Esther to save His people, who were also her people.

The Book of Nehemiah ends the historical storyline of the Old Testament.

One other book, simply titled Job, is the story of a man who suffered some of the most horrendous losses one might ever experience in a lifetime. In one day, all ten of his children died. All the oxen, sheep, and camels of his sprawling ranch, along with the servants tending them, perished in the most unique and bizarre ways. Then, he suffered a severe physical attack on his body that took him to a place just short of death itself. The story is a record of his struggle to keep his faith intact through it all.

The life of Job and all that he had to endure, pulls the curtain back to take us behind the scenes and show us a dialog between God and Satan regarding what is happening to Job. It becomes very clear that Satan is behind all the evil that Job is experiencing. Men and women of all generations have been required to face pain, suffering and loss to some degree. This book gives us a peek into the spiritual battle that is raging behind the details of the lives we live, even though we may be oblivious to it all. Here we get a glimpse into the spiritual battle of what some have called The Great Controversy between Christ and Satan. The Bible provides a broad-view perspective of this universal spiritual battle, whereas the Book of Job is a case study of that conflict through the life of one man.

After Israel returns from exile and the temple is restored, the Biblical record of the nation of Israel goes silent for approximately four hundred years. Of course life went on in Judah and around the world, but none of it is recorded in the Bible.

Some wonder why the Bible does not record the history of the other nations of the world that were in existence at the very same time. Why are they not mentioned? The Bible is focused on the sacred account of God's activity in history only as it relates to saving mankind from the penalty of death which took effect as the result of the disobedience in the Garden of Eden. The Bible is not a book of world history. It was written only for the purpose of giving insight as to where the brokenness and sin in the world comes from, and to display God's diligent effort in response to the condition of the human race.

During the four centuries between the return of the nation of Judah after their exile in Babylon until the New Testament, we know that Greece conquered the nation of Persia. We know that Rome then conquered Greece and was the occupying force in the nation of Israel at the time the record picks back up again in the New Testament. However, these historical events are recorded outside of the Bible narrative.

At this point in the story, approximately four thousand years have passed since Adam and Eve ate the fruit on that fateful day. On that very day, God promised someone would come to crush the enemy and make things right again. Without a Savior to intervene, human life would just be a blip in time and after death, each person would be gone forever. The world was still waiting for the promised one to show up and bless all the families on the earth.

God's timing is perfect. The time had come. Everything was ready and the portrayal of God in action on behalf of mankind picks up again in what we call the New Testament. Now the promised one arrives to take the center stage of history.

GOD WANTS US TO REMEMBER:

- God loves His creation and is only and totally motivated by love. That love allows the people He created to make their own choices about Him without force or coercion. When His people, Israel, continually chose to turn their back on Him and do life without Him, He let them experience their own negative consequences, which was the total destruction of their nation. God does not stand in the way of the results of the choices we make.

- God is holy, just and good, meaning He can make no mistakes. We may not understand everything that God allowed Israel and Judah to experience, but we can be sure it was not His original plan had they followed His leading in their lives.

- No individual who wants to be safe with God, and saved by Him, will be ignored. God never excludes or condemns one who wants to be in relationship with Him. God knows every heart, and we may be assured that should we see history through His eyes, we would recognize His continual fair judgments in all things.

- God sends warning after warning to us. His prophets appealed to the nations regarding the coming consequences, but they were continually ignored. Finally, God allowed them to fully experience what life without Him would be like. Choices do indeed have consequences.

"And she will have a son, and you are to name him Jesus, for he will save his people from their sins."

MATTHEW 1:21

"Don't be afraid! I bring you good news that will bring great joy to all people. The Savior—yes, the Messiah, the Lord—has been born in Bethlehem, the city of David!"

LUKE 2:10,11

When Simeon the priest saw the baby Jesus, he said, 'Sovereign Lord, now let your servant die in peace, as you have promised. I have seen your salvation, which you have prepared for all people. He is a light to reveal God to the nations, and he is the glory of your people Israel.'"

LUKE 2:29-32

10

FINALLY! HE'S HERE!

For many people, Christmas is their favorite time of the year. And it is a great time. We all know that Christmas isn't really about Santa Claus, trees, lights and Christmas gifts. Sure, those are fun things. Families and friends gather together and there is a sweet spirit in the air. Children are giddy with excitement. I fully understand that for some who don't get to enjoy any of these things, it is the hardest time of the year, and I do not want to minimize that in any way.

However, may we never forget that Christmas is really the celebration of the birth of the one who was to bless all the nations on the earth.

We know that Jesus was not born on December 25, but since we don't know the date of His actual birth, that date has been chosen for a variety of reasons. What a great event to celebrate. It has been called the greatest story ever told.

The Old Testament spans four thousand years of history, speaking about, prophesying about, and looking forward to the coming of the Savior.

The four books at the beginning of the New Testament, Matthew, Mark, Luke and John all share a short biography of the life of Jesus Christ. They are called the Gospels, or the Good News. They declare the story of the arrival of the One who was promised way back in Eden and who would provide the picture of what God wanted us to know about Him.

Why has this one birth held its grip on the world for over two thousand years?

It is sung about with majestic music. It is dramatized in amateur as well as professional settings. Countless children have played the parts of angels, Joseph, Mary, shepherds or wisemen in school plays, concerts, and church events. There are a myriad of books written about the birth, and life of Jesus.

It is estimated that over three hundred and fifty texts in the Old Testament predict the coming of the one who would crush the enemy and bring about the restoration of all that was lost in Eden. It is amazing that the life and death of Jesus Christ fulfills every one of them. That type of accuracy surely requires our attention.

In these prophetic texts, we are told what the promised One would accomplish. We find references to His birth, life, and to His manner of death. The Book of Daniel specifically informs us of the timing of his arrival, and the prophet Micah told us that he would be born in Bethlehem.

If you have heard about Jesus, but don't really know anything about Him, let me introduce Him to you.

Beginning with the manner of His conception and His birth, His life was unlike any other. Just imagine! He was born to a young girl, who was a virgin. No matter how many times you read that and scratch your head in wonderment, it is a true statement! Here is how it happened.

His mother, Mary, a young teenaged girl, lived in Nazareth, a small town in Northern Israel. One day an angel from Heaven stopped by for a visit. Now there's an event that doesn't happen every day! He had a very important message, specifically for her. "Mary, don't be frightened. God has decided to bless you. You are going to become pregnant and have a son. When he is born, name him Jesus. He will rule over Israel forever, and his kingdom will never end."

To no one's surprise, Mary asked the obvious question, "But how can I have a baby? I am a virgin?"

The angel had a ready answer and said, "God the Holy Spirit will come to you, and a miraculous life will be planted within you. The Son of God is going to be born as a normal human being, and you have been chosen to be His mother. The baby born to you will be Holy."

There you have it. That is how a virgin can give birth to a baby! It's a miraculous conception. The God who created life out of dust can also create embryonic life in the womb of a young woman. Miracles have no explanation, nor do they need to. In this case, a young woman, about to be married, was chosen to give birth to a child, without ever being with a man. That's pretty unique all by itself.

When Mary told Joseph, her fiancé, that she was going to have a baby, he went into shock and started making plans to call off the wedding. Can we blame him? However, he was a kind man and was making plans to do it quietly rather than make a public spectacle of Mary.

Thankfully, the angel who spoke to Mary also visited Joseph to offer him some perspective and much needed reassurance. He said, "Do not be afraid to go ahead with your marriage to Mary. For the child within her has been conceived by the Holy Spirit. She will have a son, and you are to name him Jesus, for he will save his people from their sins." There it is again. Conceived by the Holy Spirit. Our minds do not grasp the magnificence of this event. This was more than a typical pregnancy or birth. It was all so beautifully supernatural.

The event by which the Son of God, took on the body of a human being is referred to as the Incarnation. Mary was a virgin who gave birth to a baby boy who was God, the Son. He chose to put aside His God qualities, and powers, so that He could go through the same birth process we all experience. He would be born as a human and live just like one of us. The reason for this will become clear.

After the reassurance of the angel, Joseph revived the wedding plans and they were married. About the time for this special baby to be born, they were required to go to Bethlehem, the town where Joseph was born, to register his name in a nationwide census. That put them in exactly the right place for this baby to be born, just as the prophet Micah had said. How many ladies would sign up to ride a donkey for four or five days, covering some ninety miles from Nazareth to Bethlehem, within days of when she was ready to give birth?

Upon arriving in Bethlehem, they found there was no place to stay. There were "No Vacancy" signs everywhere. Joseph had not made advanced reservations, so they settled into a stable that was offered by the innkeeper. It may have only been a shelter for cattle, sheep and donkeys, but it was out of the wind and provided a much-needed place to rest. This is where the promised baby was born. Nothing sterile, no midwife or doctor present. Only a young woman, far away from her mother, giving birth to her first child. The one to boil the water and oversee the great event was a young husband, a carpenter by trade, who likely had not attended any pre-natal classes and knew very little if anything at all about delivering a baby.

This was the Savior promised to Adam and Eve in Eden. This was the One through whom all families of the earth would be blessed who was promised to Abraham, Isaac and Jacob. This was the Child born for a wondrous and holy purpose as predicted by the angel to Mary. This was the One the angel told Joseph would save his people from their sins. The Son of God was here.

At that same time, on a hillside not far away, an angel appeared to a group of shepherds and told them about the baby in the hay manger. They called it "Good news, of great joy for everyone! The Savior—yes the Messiah, the Lord has been born in Bethlehem tonight…this is how you will recognize him; you will find a baby lying in a manger, wrapped snugly in strips of cloth." Then suddenly, the sky was filled by a host of angels singing, "Glory to God in the highest heaven, and peace on earth to all whom God favors." The shepherds quickly ran to see the child in the manger and left praising God that they had seen the child who had been prophesied about for so many centuries.

It is obvious that this Child, to be named Jesus, is someone who deserves our attention. Jesus' name is often used as a curse word, but the Bible calls him Holy! His conception is miraculous, His birth is special, and all of Heaven became energized to share the good news. We also learn about wise men from far Eastern countries who knew about this child from their study of prophetic writings. They made the long journey and arrived to worship Him, bringing expensive gifts. Mary and Joseph must have wondered what would happen next.

God wanted to get close to us. He could not come as God in His fullness because we would not be able to stand in His presence. He is holy, and we are not. Through Adam and Eve we turned away from Him way back in Eden and have been hiding ever since. We do not have what it takes to bring about a reset of what was lost all on our own. But God had a plan, and this was just the beginning. This baby is divinity wrapped in humanity. God in a human body, kicking, laughing, crying, helpless, even needing his diapers changed and dependent on the milk of his mother to survive!

After His birth, we don't know much about Jesus for the next thirty years. We know that He lived in Egypt for two years when angels told Joseph and Mary to go there to avoid the irrational anger of King Herod who wanted to kill the child the people referred to as a king.

We also know that at the age of twelve, He had a very lengthy, deep discussion with learned teachers in the temple at Jerusalem about topics of God and Heaven. When His parents reprimanded Him for not telling them where He was, He simply informed them that He was just going about His Father's business.

The life of Jesus was simple. His earthly father, Joseph, was a carpenter in Nazareth. Jesus took up the trade as well, learning the skills from him. The creator of trees was now cutting trees, sanding and assembling wood pieces with his hands to make chairs and tables and bed frames. I like to imagine what it was like to work alongside Jesus. I can only believe that His work was careful, measured, and precise. His finished products must have been masterpieces. I wonder if He hit His thumb with a hammer and if so, how He responded. Did He scrape his fingers and need bandages? He was human, experiencing the life each of us live.

Years went by, and when Jesus turned thirty years of age, everything in His life changed. He left the carpenter shop in Nazareth and arrived at the Jordan River where His first cousin, John the Baptist, was preaching and baptizing people. John recognized Him for who He was and pointed Him out to the crowd and said, "Behold, the lamb of God who takes away the sin of the world."

From the time of Adam and Eve, worship and repentance involved the sacrifice of a living creature, usually a lamb. As grisly as the ritual sounds, the symbolism is rich. God was teaching that the automatic, natural result of sin is death. By bringing a living sacrifice, the meaning behind the ritual taught that sin is a serious matter, causing death, but not the death of the one confessing the sin. As people brought their lambs and confessed their sin by placing their hands on its head, they were acknowledging that their life was spared by the death of another.

As shocking as the act of sacrificing an innocent lamb must have been, the message is that sin, turning our back on God, was a horrific, rebellious act against Him. His peaceful loving universe was eternally disrupted. Mankind's disobedience was no small thing to God, but He loved us all so deeply He designed a way to save us and restore all things.

The people didn't know Jesus, the one John was pointing to, but they understood the symbolism very well. The "lamb taking away sin" was common everyday language for them.

Jesus then asked John to baptize Him, so John took Him down into the river and did as He asked. As they came up out of the water, the Holy Spirit, in the form of a dove, fluttered down and rested on Jesus. Then a voice was heard from Heaven saying, "This is my dearly loved Son, who brings me great joy." Other versions say, "This is my beloved Son, in whom I am well pleased." (NASB) Matthew 3:17

This was a total endorsement of Jesus by God the Father Himself.

Jesus was determined to live His life by one single principle, which was to only do that which was directed by God, His Father. He was totally submissive to the Father's guidance in every aspect of His life. This was a total contrast to the decision made by Adam and Eve when they chose to do the exact opposite of what God had asked of them.

Right after His baptism, Jesus was led into the wilderness by the Holy Spirit, where He fasted for forty days and nights. He was alone with God. After almost six weeks without food, we can appreciate that He would be very hungry, and very weak.

The enemy who came to Eve at the tree in the Garden of Eden decided to use this moment of His fragility to come to Jesus with his tantalizing, philosophical temptations. It was the enemy's goal to see if just as he had done with Eve, maybe he could also get Jesus to shift His loyalty from His Father over to himself. He tempted Jesus in three different ways, in rather quick succession.

First, when Jesus was absolutely famished, he said, "If you really are the Son of God, tell these stones to become loaves of bread." Notice his tantalizing challenge. "If you really are the Son of God." He was appealing to Jesus' ego to see if He would react to his challenge and prove Himself to be God's Son. Just perform this miracle to make it clear who you are, and while you're at it, solve your hunger crisis at the same time. Jesus replied that the Bible says that we don't live just on bread alone, but also on every word that comes from the mouth of God. He was making it clear that He would eat when His Father would direct Him to eat, not when He wanted to eat, and certainly not when the enemy told Him to eat. He passed that test.

Next, the enemy took Him to the pinnacle of the temple in Jerusalem and said, "If you are the Son of God, go ahead and jump from here for the Scripture says that angels will hold you up and protect you, so that you won't even hurt your foot." And again, Jesus quoted Scripture and reminded Satan that the Scripture also says that we are to never test the Lord your God. He passed test number two.

The enemy tried one more time. He took Jesus to a very high mountain and opened before His eyes all the kingdoms of the world and the history laid out into the future and said, "I'll give you all this if you just kneel down and worship me." Remember that when Satan tempted Eve and Adam and they gave him their loyalty, he became the de facto ruler of the world. Jesus even referred to him as such. So, because Satan had not yet been defeated, he had a right to offer things from the world to Jesus in return for worship.

Steadfast and true, Jesus once again quoted Scripture in His response and said, "The Scripture says, 'You must worship the LORD your God and serve only him.'" He passed the final test. With that the devil left Him, a defeated foe. All the details are recorded in Matthew 4:1-11

At this time the angels of Heaven came to Jesus and brought food to nourish and strengthen Him as He prepared for the life and work ahead of Him.

Adam and Eve had failed when tempted by the devil back in Eden. Jesus was met head on, in a very frail condition due to his recent fasting, but He squarely faced the enemy and stood strong. The enemy withdrew, but he was not done with Jesus yet. He was more determined than ever to come back as many times as it would take and to use any angle necessary in order to get Jesus to make one single mistake. All he had to do was to get Jesus to let go of His commitment to be only guided by His Father. Even if he could get Him to react in frustration or anger, that would be all he would need. Just once! If that happened, it would mean that no one, not even God Himself, was able to withstand Satan and his work.

GOD WANTS US TO REMEMBER:

- God always keeps His promises. He said He would send one to crush the serpent. He said He would send one to bless all the nations of the earth. The centuries-long wait was finally over, and One called the Son of God was born to enter our world so that the promises would all come true.

- The miraculous nature of His conception, the unique circumstances of His birth being in the exact place that had been prophesied hundreds of years before, and the announcement of His birth by heavenly angels all speak to the working of God in the world through the life of His Son.

- God desperately wants us to know the truth about His character and who He is. It was so important to Him that God the Son came to live among us. He took the human name Jesus when He was born to Mary, and became one of us so that He could talk our language, be close to us, and identify with our pain. More importantly He wanted us to experience His loving heart in an up close and personal way.

- The wilderness temptation experience where Jesus met every enticement of the devil with a response straight from the Old Testament informs us that Jesus, the Son of God, trusted the Scripture as His guiding light. He demonstrated total commitment to follow the words and principles that are contained there. He must have believed the Scripture He had learned was true.

This simple children's song says it all:

Jesus loves me, this I know.
For the Bible tells me so.
Little ones to Him belong.
They are weak, but He is strong.
Yes, Jesus loves me.
Yes, Jesus loves me.
Yes, Jesus loves me.
The Bible tells me so.

11

THE WAY GOD LOVES

After overcoming the enemy's temptation, Jesus began to travel about the land of Israel, teaching, preaching and performing miracles in order to inform us about and to demonstrate God's love for us all. The last verse in the Book of John says, "I suppose that if all the other things Jesus did were written down, the whole world could not contain the books." A stunning statement to demonstrate the impact He had made on His friends as well as to also give us a window into the awe and respect that Jesus' contemporaries had for Him.

Jesus lived a life that was totally focused on others. In this way, He didn't just speak about love or define it in words, He continually demonstrated that real love is always other-centered.

We read about how he healed lame people so they could walk.

He opened blind eyes so they could see.

He touched lepers, which was a social taboo, and made their flesh whole and new again.

He healed all manner of diseases, sickness and fevers.

He made deaf people hear and He cast demons out of possessed, frantic people, leaving them calm and in their right minds.

Can you imagine waiting in line for your turn to stand in front of Jesus and tell Him about whatever pain or disease you struggled with, and walk away healed and rejoicing? How wonderfully amazing!

The most impressive miracles would no doubt be the times when He brought people back to life after they had died. The one that receives the most attention is what happened when His good friend Lazarus died. Jesus arrived at the home of Mary and Martha, Lazarus' sisters, after Lazarus had been dead for four days. He saw their grief and wanted to be taken to see where Lazarus had been buried. He asked that they roll the stone away from the tomb but the sisters protested, fearing the odor from the body would be too much. Jesus insisted, and when the stone was rolled back, He then called into the tomb for Lazarus to come out. It's my guess that no one moved or breathed for the next several seconds as all eyes were riveted on the opening of that tomb! And then, there he was! Lazarus came out alive and well. It was a common Jewish belief that only the Messiah, the Savior, would be able to raise someone from the dead after three days. Jesus had just done it, and no doubt the word about this event spread like fire through dry stubble.

We read the details of all Jesus' miracles in the first four books of the New Testament, and since the Bible records only a sampling of what He did, there are no doubt countless accounts of the same types of stories that we have no knowledge of.

However, Jesus didn't come to just perform miracles. He came to be WITH us, walk with us and experience life in our human, degenerated state. He didn't take on the health and statuesque marvel of a newly created Adam, He took on human flesh in the strength and stature of many centuries of declined health and strength. His ultimate mission was to love us in ways that no one else could. In John's book about Jesus, he simply said, "So the Word (another name for Jesus) became human and made his home among us." John 1:14

The relationship that God designed for us at the time of creation was lost. The human heart craves connection, a relationship with at least one person where it is safe to be honest, vulnerable and real. A friend where one can proclaim by word or action that, "This is who I am, this is all of me, including the brokenness and ugliness of my life," and find that that friend stays by even through the good and the bad times. Even when the "who I am" is confused, completely disoriented and fearful of what lies ahead.

Jesus made His home among us in order to be that friend for each of us. He met people in their messiest, sinful moments and loved them despite their brokenness, much to the dismay of those who considered themselves righteous and much more worthy of God's love.

One time the religious teachers wanted to back him into a corner and set up a trap they were sure would be successful. They brought a woman to Him who had been "caught in the act of adultery." They challenged Him by asking what they should do with her. "Our law says we should stone her, what do you say?"

Jesus immediately recognized the trap. If He said yes, go ahead, He would be taking on the role of the Roman nation who was occupying Israel at the time, and who reserved that only they had the right of judgment and administration of the death penalty. If He said no, He would be accused of despising the Jewish laws of Moses which they honored. They thought it was the perfect hook for Jesus to hang Himself on.

His wisdom saw through it all and He said, "Alright, (meaning go ahead and stone her) but let the one who has never sinned cast the first stone!" With that, He began to write in the sand with His finger. Many believe He was writing a list of the sins and actions of those who were presently standing there accusing the woman. Suddenly, as they observed what He wrote and recognized their own hypocrisy, they all crept away as if they suddenly remembered they had urgent appointments in other places.

Finally, Jesus said to the woman, "Where are your accusers? Didn't even one of them condemn you?" She answered "No, Lord."

Then He said two very significant things. "Neither do I. Go and sin no more."

He knew her soul. He knew she was guilty of adultery, and He was not ignoring that. He knew that maybe she was just trying to make enough money to purchase her next meal, or possibly just seeking someone to love her and make her feel cherished. Either way, it was not getting her what she wanted, and she likely didn't have a high level of self-esteem when she looked in the mirror. He wanted her to know that He loved her and had no condemnation of her. He also wanted more for her when He appealed to her, "Go and sin no more." He knew that she would never be at peace or experience the joy He wanted her to have if she continued in that lifestyle. He isn't nearly as concerned about our past as much as He is passionately interested in our future. No matter where we have been in life it is His desire that we finish well.

Once Jesus healed a lame man who had been suffering for thirty-eight years. After healing the man, Jesus said to him, "Now you are well; so stop sinning, or something worse may happen to you."

Jesus is very gracious to find people and love them where they are at, but He never wants to leave us where He finds us. He wants us to grow. He wants us to experience and enjoy the abundant life that comes when we engage in and participate in a relationship with Him. He had many encounters with people who were often considered the trash and sinners of society by those with a judgmental or critical mindset. It is recorded, that on more than one occasion, He went to gatherings for a meal with a group of prostitutes, tax collectors and those who were often considered "less than". We might even call them parties. He was accused of associating with them, to which he answered, "Yes, I do spend time with them. That's why I came." He added, "Healthy people don't need a doctor—sick people do. I have come to call not those who think they are righteous, but those who know they are sinners." Mark 2:17

Through His miracles, His tenderness and gentleness with people, His instruction to show us the best tools for life, He always had only one ultimate goal. The mission on His mind, that which brought Him here to make His home among us, was to let people know the truth about the loving character of His Father. He wanted us to know about

His Father's desire to heal us of our sinful condition and to bring about the restoration of all things that had been lost, including our hearts.

Just like today, people in Jesus' time had views of God that were skewed and misinformed. One time Jesus and his disciples passed a man, who had been born blind, sitting beside the road. They asked Jesus, "Was this man born this way because he was a sinner or because his parents were sinners?" Their view was that God punishes some people with blindness at birth because they were going to be a sinner after they were born, or because the parents who gave him birth needed to be punished for sins they had committed before the child was even born. Jesus corrected their view of God and then went on to heal the man and gave him his eyesight, so that he could now see for the first time in his life.

The lame man who had been laying by a pool for thirty-eight years, believed like many others, that when the water suddenly stirred, if he was the first in the pool he would be healed. It was a myth. Rippling water was not God's sign of an imminent miracle. On this day, Jesus simply walked right up to him as if He went there for this purpose only, asked him if he would like to get well, and then healed him. No magic or mysterious water stirrings. The man stood up and walked home carrying the mat he had been sleeping on all those many years.

As wonderful as His miracles, teachings and love are, His claim to be able to forgive sins is the best gift of all. This is the deepest cry of the human heart. We are not able to undo the human condition we are born in. We cannot go back and redo the choices we have made that have hurt ourselves and others as a result of this condition. We need restoration from God Himself, and we need a renewed heart.

One time Jesus was speaking to a group of people who had gathered in a house with many people pressing into the room to hear Him. There was no way to even get close to the door because of the crowd standing around outside trying to listen through the open windows. A paralyzed man was carried there by four friends bringing him to Jesus for healing. When they could not get in, they went up on the roof, broke up the tiles and with ropes lowered him and the cot he was laying on down into the middle of the very room where Jesus stood teaching.

Jesus recognized that the effort of these men who would go to such extremes on behalf of their friend was because of the faith they had in Him. He turned to the man on the mat and said, "My child, your sins are forgiven."

This caused quite a stir. The people standing there listening to Him quickly reacted, asking, "What is He saying? Who does He think He is! This is blasphemy! Only God can forgive sins!"

Jesus could read their thoughts, so He asked them, "Why do you question this in your hearts? Is it easier to say to the paralyzed man 'Your sins are forgiven,' or 'Stand up, pick up your mat, and walk?'" So I will prove to you that the Son of Man has the authority on Earth to forgive sins." Then He turned to the paralyzed man and said, 'Stand up, pick up your mat, and go home!"

The man jumped up, rolled up his mat, and headed for the door as they pressed back to make way for him to walk out through the crowd. It had been too crowded for him to get into the room, but a lame man walking with poles over his shoulder was able to cut a wide path on the way out! The people were amazed, praising God.

When Jesus said, "Your sins are forgiven," there would be no physical proof that his sins were actually forgiven. So, it would be easy to say that. However, to say "Get up and walk" was very different. The proof of His ability to do that would be very evident. When He said that to the man, who was immediately healed and walked out, Jesus tied the two items together. He was saying, "I will prove to you I have the authority to forgive his sins by healing this man's lame legs."

No one except Jesus has ever even offered, let alone demonstrated, that He has the authority to forgive sins. Jesus Christ is the only One who has the answer for humanity's dilemma. He is the Conqueror on our behalf against the bullying enemy.

Along with showing us His power and His personal interest in us by His actions, Jesus also taught us through His words. He spoke in parables, which were stories that had a double meaning. On the surface, one could say He spoke fables and cute little anecdotes. But there was always something deeper, something with a spiritual application behind each parable He spoke.

For example, He talked about a man who dug up a treasure while he was plowing his employer's field. He quickly buried the treasure again, then went home and sold everything he owned to raise enough money to purchase the field. Then he promptly bought the field, along with the buried treasure. That was it. It could simply be written off as a fable.

The deeper meaning that Jesus wanted us to see was that when we find the treasure of the meaning of life, or the truth about who God is, we will sacrifice anything necessary in order to experience the personal benefit of it for ourselves.

Jesus told many parables, giving simple, logical presentations about how to live the best life possible. The greatest address He ever gave is found in the book of Matthew, chapters five through seven. It is often referred to as the Sermon on the Mount, and I like to think of it as the "Manifesto" of what it means to be a follower of Jesus.

In this sermon He spoke about things such as how to be a good influence in a dark world. How to forgive others, and how to live without worry.

He spoke about how lust and anger are heart issues long before any actions are taken.

Here He taught us how to pray, and about the hold possessions can have on our hearts.

Some of the hardest things He taught in this sermon include the need to love all people, including our enemies. He told us the importance and power of forgiveness.

Those are challenging principles, but He didn't just teach them. He demonstrated everything He taught in the life He lived every day. People who choose to orient their lives around these principles are changed, peaceful, and become the mentors we find ourselves looking up to in life. They stand out in a crowd.

He counseled us to take care of the needy, and this is where the golden rule is found. "Do to others whatever you would like them to do to you."

He also reminded us about the destruction that comes from judging others. He reminded us that we are all human, and we should not forget that when we look down upon or condemn someone else. He said, "Why worry about a speck in your friend's eye when you have a log in your own?" Matthew 7:3 When we observe the life and personality of Jesus, He is an example of a man to look up to and be assured that we will never go wrong if we live as He lived.

This is just a small sampling of His wisdom that He shared with all of us. He claimed to be God wrapped in human skin and bones. His heavenly thoughts and wisdom left people speechless. They marveled and commented to each other that "Never a man spoke like this man." We are better people and have more satisfying relationships with everyone we meet when we follow His principles for life.

Just like His conception and birth were evidence of divine involvement, His life and teachings were far beyond any religious teacher before or since. His life is like no other.

Many biographies devote most of the pages and space to the lives and legacies of the one being written about, and then quickly refer to their death at the end. Here we find the reverse. It is intriguing that more time is spent talking about the death of Jesus than is spent talking about His life. That's because His death was His legacy, and that which He is remembered for most of all. It's His death that changed everything for every human on the planet. "Through Him all the nations of the earth will be blessed."

Because of Jesus, we are all blessed, and also because of Him, the best is yet to come!

GOD WANTS US TO REMEMBER:

- Jesus' life was not typical in many ways. He shared profound wisdom. He proved He could heal. He proved He could raise people from the dead. He was the God who came to live among us so He could walk with us, sit beside us, love us. He went out of his way to show love to the "scum" and the ignored, unpopular people of society. He did everything He could possibly do to prove that He was the promised One. The Messiah.

- God's love is much deeper, broader, and fuller than human love, as was demonstrated through the life of Jesus. As we personally experience that loving relationship with Him it draws out of us the best kind of love that we could ever have to pass on to others.

God loves people just the way they are, but He loves them too much to leave them that way.

MAX LUCADO

Everyone has a love story. It's the Bible. It tells you how much God loves you and how far He went to win your heart.

ANONYMOUS

If you feel you don't deserve God's love, you're right—but that's good news because God's love never depends on your performance or accomplishments.

ANONYMOUS

12

A CRUCIFIED KING

The Biblical books of Matthew, Mark, Luke and John are referred to as the "Gospels," which simply means "the good news." It was good news that the One the world had waited for so long had finally arrived. It was good news that He could forgive sins. It was good news that He could set the record straight about the character and love of God.

The picture of Jesus that emerges captures the life of a man on a mission. He was not just born to live out an ordinary life. He arrived with a passion and full commitment for the purpose He came to fulfill.

Even at the age of twelve He reminded His mother that she should not be surprised that He would be doing His Father's business. He was focused.

His friends wanted Him to do or say things that would reveal the truth about Himself, and who He really was. They recognized that He was the promised One, the Messiah, and they urged Him to make that known. To broadcast it far and wide. His simple response was always the same, "My time has not yet come."

He fully understood He was here to fulfill prophecy, and that He was the promised blessing the world was waiting for, but He was determined to have it all play out on God the Father's timeline. He trusted His Father to guide Him in every aspect, including the timing of His life.

Later on however, we notice that His words changed completely. He was thirty-three years old. His miracles, His teachings, as well as

His activities had been the center of attention, the gossip of the nation for about three and a half years. Many people loved Him for His simple teachings and His gentleness to them, but many more people hated Him because He threatened the status quo of their religious norms. These people were more focused on the rules and keeping score of what one had to accomplish for God in order to be accepted by God.

Jesus came to show us that God's love and acceptance is already in place. From there He taught us how to live lives that would allow us to enjoy God's love, not focused or striving on how to earn it.

In the year 31 A.D., Jesus was in Jerusalem during the week of the Passover festival. The Hebrew people had celebrated this feast each year in commemoration of that last night in Egypt where blood on the doorposts was the signal to the death angel to pass over their home. Jesus wanted to celebrate this supper ritual with His disciples and said to them, "As you go into the city you will see a certain man. Tell him, 'The Teacher says: My time has come, and I will eat the Passover meal with my disciples at your house.'" Matthew 26:18

Did you catch it? "My time has come." This was new.

When they arrived at the room where they were to eat together, there was no servant waiting for them. Typically, there would be someone who would welcome them, and then perform a rather earthy service to them by washing the feet of each guest. After walking to the place of supper their sandaled feet would surely be dusty, and it was the servant's job to wash the dust off and refresh their feet before the evening's events.

The disciples often argued among themselves about which one of them was the greatest, and "the greatest" would never stoop to wash someone else's feet! There was no way any of them were going to do it. Jesus got the basin, the water, wrapped a towel around His waist and got down on His knees to wash all the disciples' hot, dusty feet. They sat in shock as He went one by one until He had served each of them. He had said that "the greatest among you is the one that is the servant."

128

He loved them all, including Judas who was about to betray Jesus to His enemies within the next few hours. Jesus was not an ordinary man.

After the meal that evening, He spent time talking with and teaching His disciples with an intensity that He had not ever displayed before. You know how it is when you are about to say good-bye to friends or family, knowing you won't see them again for a while. With our hand on the doorknob, we pause and move to a place of relationship depth that we never reached at any time during the visit. "Don't forget this . . ." "Remember to . . ." "I just want to assure you about . . ."

This was Jesus' "hand on the doorknob" moment with those who had followed Him around for these three and a half years. He wanted to make sure He did not forget any last, urgent concerns. Finally, after He was finished teaching them, He prayed a prayer to His Father that is recorded in John 17, where He said that He had completed the work He came to do. "I taught them, I protected them, and I gave them Your word. I have finished My work." Then even to His Father He makes it clear that He knows "my time has come."

Time for what?

After supper, He and His disciples went out to a familiar retreat setting called the Garden of Gethsemane (Geth-sem-an-ee). It was at the end of a long day. He had talked long with His disciples at the Passover meal. His words had been intense and passionate. He had told them He would need to go away for a time but promised He would come back to them. He had not said things like this to them before. They were startled and fearful, probably even a bit disoriented.

As they all found places to rest in the garden, Jesus asked them to stay awake and pray for themselves and for Him. After that He took Peter, James and John, His three closest companions, and went deeper into the recesses of the garden. He again asked them to pray for Him. Then, He went off alone, and they heard Him cry out in a desperate voice "Father, if you are willing, please take this cup of suffering away from me. Yet I want your will to be done, not mine." Luke 22:42 He was in a state of such agony that His sweat came out and fell as if they were great drops of blood.

As always, He only wanted to do what God wanted from Him.

Eventually, He staggered back to be with His friends and found them all sound asleep. He woke them up, once again pleading with them to pray for Him, and then retreated back to where He had been before. Falling to His knees He once again repeated the same agonizing request to His Father. That scenario repeated itself three times.

There was something terrifying about this experience. The disciples had never seen Him looking or acting like this, and they were alarmed. In their exhaustion, they fell asleep, even while praying as Jesus had asked. They certainly did not understand what this "cup of suffering" was that Jesus wanted to avoid, but it was clear that He was committed to His Father's will about it. The whole scene was surreal to them. It seemed to them that they were watching the Son of God experience a mental breakdown right in front of their eyes.

When Jesus was done praying He woke all the disciples up to tell them it was time to go. As they were leaving the garden, they were met by a rowdy mob who were being led by Judas, one of His own disciples. Judas had just been with Jesus and all the others as they had eaten the Passover meal. Jesus had washed his feet. However, Judas had a sinister purpose and left the meal early to make a deal with those who wanted to kill Jesus. For a payment of thirty pieces of silver, he had agreed to lead them to Jesus because it was at night, and they didn't want to lose track of Him or let Him out of their sight when He was so close. Judas went right up to Jesus and kissed Him on the cheek, which was the signal to these thugs as to exactly which one they were to arrest.

They quickly surrounded Jesus, tied His hands and led Him away. The disciples scattered into the darkness like scared rabbits, terrified that they might also be arrested because of their association with Jesus.

The mob led Jesus to the home of Annas, the high priest. The high priest was the one who oversaw the leading of worship services and sacrifices at the temple. His official role was a spiritual one, not political, but tonight he was on a mission to eliminate this Jesus who was very popular among the people. Tonight, he was motivated by the darkest part of the human heart, jealousy and revenge. He, along with his supporters, were threatened because it seemed to them that the actions of Jesus along with the things He taught, undermined the rules, regulations and trusted traditions that they held onto so tightly.

There was not a moment of sleep for Jesus that night. He was accused, taunted, and made fun of in the courtyard of the high priest's home. He was mocked and ridiculed as His words were taken out of context, then thrown back at Him. Most of His disciples had disappeared, leaving Him all alone with this riotous crowd.

Earlier in the evening, Peter, one of Jesus' closest friends, had vowed he would never leave Jesus and would stand up for Him no matter what might happen to Him. Jesus, looking directly at him, sadly stated that in fact Peter would deny Him three times that night before the rooster crowed in the morning. Peter had not run like the others but bravely followed Jesus right into the courtyard where the mob led Him. There he hid in the shadows, hoping to go unnoticed. However, when he was recognized, he was questioned about being with Jesus. In fear, Peter kept denying that he even knew Jesus, and when challenged again because of his Galilean speech, he vehemently disclaimed any relationship with Jesus, emphasizing his lie by swearing.

Suddenly, a rooster crowed nearby, jolting Peter's memory. Startled by the sound he sadly realized that Jesus knew Him better than he even knew himself. Peter bolted, running out into the night, weeping in anger and bitterness at himself, full of regret and embarrassment.

Jesus was rushed to a quickly assembled gathering of the highest court in the nation. They confronted Him, charging that He had claimed to be the Son of God, reminding Him that claiming to be God was blasphemy. In their minds, this was more than enough reason to have Him put to death.

However, being under the occupation of the Roman Empire, the nation of Israel was not independent at that time. They could enact their own laws of worship, ceremonies and culture, but the local governors of Rome were the only ones who could punish anyone or sentence them to death.

The mob marched Jesus off to stand in front of Pilate, the Roman governor stationed there. Pilate was not even remotely interested in getting involved in a personality or religious dispute of this magnitude, and to his delight, discovered that Jesus was from Nazareth in Galilee, a few miles North of Jerusalem. Pilate knew that Herod Antipas, the ruler over Galilee, coincidentally just happened to be in Jerusalem that night. Breathing a sigh of relief, he sidestepped the issue and sent Jesus over to see Herod.

Pilate sent a message to Herod saying that in his eyes Jesus was innocent. Herod was delighted to see this Jesus, whom he had heard so much about, but Jesus was very quiet and did not respond to his scoffing questions. Herod even challenged Jesus to perform a miracle for him to prove that He was who He said He was, but Jesus refused. His miracles were not to be on display like circus or magical acts. Herod, and the soldiers nearby, began to ridicule Jesus, putting a purple robe on Him, mocking His claim that He was the king of the Jews.

They never did understand that Jesus' claim of kingship was speaking in spiritual perspective only. He saw Himself as a King, for sure, but never once claimed that He would be a political king, ruling over their land.

The concept of what the Messiah would accomplish when He arrived had been evolving for centuries. It had morphed into a belief which included that the coming Messiah would free the people of Israel from the Roman occupation they were experiencing. However, Jesus knew that wasn't His calling and was instead aware that He was coming to be the King of the Kingdom of God, providing safety and security for people's spiritual needs. So, Jesus remained silent. After tiring of the silence, Herod sent Him back to Pilate with a message saying that he too believed Jesus had done nothing that deserved the death penalty.

Pilate talked with Jesus again, finally saying to the priests and leading elders nearby that he found Jesus to be innocent, guilty of nothing requiring death. They panicked, thinking that Jesus was going to go free when they had Him right there in their hands. To hopefully appease them, Pilate agreed to have Jesus beaten and then set free. Interesting conclusion which lacks even basic logic! "He's innocent, but for your sake I'll beat Him before I let Him go."

The murderous crowd increased in size, screaming out their insistence that Jesus be crucified. Pilate lost his nerve. Not wanting to have to deal with this kind of unrest, and fearing for his future, he relented, releasing Jesus to them with the sentence that He was to be crucified. He had Jesus beaten, and to mock His claim one more time of being a king, the soldiers put the purple robe back on Him and pressed a crown of thorns into His head as another way to make fun of His claim of being a king.

They led Jesus through the streets of Jerusalem, out of town to a place called Calvary, where crucifixions took place. After being up all night and with the loss of blood from the beating, He was too weak to carry His own cross and fell under the weight of it. A stranger, who just happened to be nearby, was forced into carrying Jesus' cross to the place of crucifixion.

There were two others who were being crucified at the same time with Jesus that day. He was not alone. They are not named; they are simply identified as two criminals. For a time, they both ridiculed and taunted Jesus. They must have heard about Jesus because one of them said, "So, you're the Messiah are you. Prove it by saving yourself—and us, too, while you're at it." The other reminded his friend that they were guilty, but it was obvious that Jesus was innocent and did not deserve punishment. Then, in complete humility he turned to Jesus and asked to be forgiven. Jesus assured him that in that moment he was forgiven, and that he would be in Heaven. Even on the cross, Jesus carried a spirit of grace and mercy for others, generously reaching out and offering it to anyone, even dying criminals, who would acknowledge their need of Him.

The Biblical record does not say much about the experience of crucifixion, but there are many accounts describing the horrific process in detail. It is hard to imagine the deep and utter cruelty of this punishment. His feet were nailed to a wooden pole and his hands were nailed to a crossbar attached to the pole. Then the cross was dropped into a hole in the ground to make it stand upright. Criminals on their crosses were raised up off the ground, stripped of their clothes and left to hang as a naked spectacle with no dignity whatsoever. Sometimes it would take a few days for people to die, suffering the heat of the day, the cold of the night, along with insects that would be attracted to their wounds. The process was agonizing in every way, for every single minute, until death finally ended their suffering. The inhumanity of it all stretches beyond our imagination.

Along with the agony of the tortured bodies, the criminals were subjected to taunts, teasing, and harassment from the crowd of onlookers who would be present. These occasions were actually a form of entertainment for some people. Without the typical devices of amusement and diversion that we are used to today, a public spectacle like this may have been the most exciting event of the day, or week. Curious onlookers were often present to take it all in.

Just as the birth of Jesus was supernatural and unique in so many ways, so also was His death. He was crucified at about nine o'clock in the morning. For three hours, He was exposed to the elements, to the bystanders, and to the rabble of the noisy crowd. Then suddenly everything went as dark as night, a totally unnatural event. At twelve noon the people were suddenly feeling their way around, unable to see anything. For this to happen right in the middle of this disgusting spectacle was extremely unsettling and disturbing. The darkness lingered for three more unnerving hours until it finally lifted at around three in the afternoon and the few remaining hours of daylight returned.

Jesus willingly went to Calvary, of His own free will. He was God! He could have easily resisted and left every single person humbled in the dust. No one wants to die, especially like this, but He was aware that this was His main purpose for being born as one of us. His ultimate mission to planet Earth was to assure sinful humans of the love God had for them, taking on Himself the penalty of death that was in fact to be our penalty.

This was the cup He had asked the Father to remove from Him. After praying and wrestling about this in Gethsemane, and not hearing of an alternative option, He accepted this plan and remained calm, composed, and submissive. There was no need for the soldiers to wrestle Him down to be nailed to the cross, nor did He rail and rant against his executioners. In fact, He prayed out loud to His Father for those who crucified him. "Father, forgive them, they don't know what they are doing." About six hours after being nailed there, Jesus finally cried out to His Father in Heaven and said, "It is finished!" With those words His head fell forward, and He died.

Along with the darkness that surrounded the cross at mid-day, two other miraculous things happened at the time of His death. The Bible records that when He died, many graves were opened. While not identified by name, the ones in those graves came back to life, and were seen walking, talking and associating with others. How unsettling would that be?

Also, there was a heavy curtain hanging in the temple that had significant meaning regarding the presence of God in their worship services. The curtain divided the Holy Place from the Most Holy Place, giving them a visual perspective on being in the presence of this Holy God. The priest would go behind that heavy curtain into the Most Holy Place only one time per year as they honored the sacredness of the presence of God in that specific place. At the very moment that Jesus died on the cross at Calvary, outside the city of Jerusalem, that curtain was mysteriously ripped apart, torn by unseen hands, starting from the top and tearing all the way to the bottom. The curtain was far too thick and heavy to be torn by human hands, nor would there be any way for someone to get to the top of the curtain where the tear began.

This torn curtain was a signal from God to humanity that there was no further need of animal sacrifices because those rituals had only been pointing ahead to the Messiah who would be the universal sacrifice for all of mankind. Just as John the Baptist had said at Jesus' baptism, Jesus was in fact "the Lamb of God who came to take away the sin of the world." He had died. The sacrifice was complete and Jesus had fulfilled His purpose. It truly was finished, just as He had said as He took His last breath.

There was a Roman soldier standing near the cross when Jesus died. He had been present for the proceedings and had been drawn to Jesus' calm demeanor through it all. Noticing that Jesus died so quickly, along with the strange darkness, and the gentle nature of Jesus as He hung there, the soldier exclaimed out loud with conviction that "this truly must have been the Son of God!"

What a horrific, repulsive ending to the life of the One who had such a unique and miraculous birth, and who claimed to be the Son of God. The supernatural events of His birth and death could not be ignored, but it simply made no sense that when He was able to do such miraculous things why He had allowed it all to end like this. He was dead. What now? The disciples gathered in a room in the city and locked the door. They were terrified, totally confused and disoriented, naturally assuming that someone would soon be looking for them as well.

A few people stayed to take care of things at the crucifixion site. There was usually a gruesome place nearby where crucified criminals' bodies were taken and dumped, without formality or respect. However, a man named Joseph asked Pilate, and was given permission, to take Jesus' body for burial in a tomb he had prepared for himself someday when he would need it. Acting with respect and treating Jesus' body with dignity, they carefully wrapped it in a linen burial cloth and carried it to Joseph's tomb to lay it reverently there. A large stone was rolled in front of the opening.

Three women followed along to discover where He would be buried so that they could come back and cover His body with embalming spices. It was late afternoon on the day before their Sabbath, which they kept as a holy day, so therefore would rest from all unnecessary activities. The ladies planned to come back to the tomb to do their work first thing the morning after the Sabbath was over. All was quiet and still in the tomb where Jesus lay.

At the appointed time, the women gathered and carried the spices they had prepared to the tomb. As they walked, they wondered who they could get to roll the stone away from the entrance that had been put in place when He was buried. Imagine their shock when they got there, only to find that the stone had already been rolled aside. In trembling fear, they stepped inside and were met by two men arrayed in dazzling white clothes. Angels! The ladies bowed their faces to the ground as they heard one of the angels say, "Why are you looking among the dead for someone who is alive? He isn't here! He has risen from the dead! Remember what He told you back in Galilee, that the Son of Man must be betrayed into the hands of sinful men and be crucified, and that He would rise again on the third day?" Luke 24:5-7

Was this a cruel joke? Were the angels taunting them?

No doubt the disciples had heard Him say those words, but they were ignored because they would not believe that Jesus would have to suffer such treatment. Now they were being reminded of what He had told them.

That same day Jesus appeared to Mary, one of His closest followers, right there near the tomb when she came to spend some time grieving His death. He asked her to go tell the disciples, and Peter, to meet Him in Galilee. He specifically added, "And Peter." Jesus wanted Peter to know that, despite his denial in the courtyard the night of Jesus' betrayal, He loved Peter and wanted to see him there too.

Later that same day, Jesus joined two individuals as they walked along a road traveling home to the small town of Emmaus. He listened as they discussed their distress over the death of Jesus who they had been sure was the Messiah. They were so deep into their discussion that they did not even recognize that it was the resurrected Jesus they were walking with and talking to. As they sat to eat, suddenly their eyes were opened. In shock they realized it was Jesus Himself who had been with them, so they quickly started back to Jerusalem in the dark to tell their friends they had seen the risen Jesus.

Jesus appeared that same evening to His close disciples, who were locked in a room in fear, to show them that He in fact had been resurrected that very morning and was very much alive.

Jesus remained on the earth after that for another forty days, meeting and talking with friends. He reminded them that He had already told them about how He would die, but that in three days He would be resurrected. They had been so sure that the Messiah would not or could not be killed that when He actually died they had forgotten what He had told them about coming back to life again.

As Jesus was talking with His disciples at the Passover meal on the night before He was crucified, He had made them a promise. He told them He would be going away, and that when He left, He would not leave them alone. He said He would not leave them like orphans and that God, the Holy Spirit would come to be with them in His place.

God the Holy Spirit is omnipresent, making Him able to be everywhere at the same time. Jesus, God the Son, had given up the ability to be omnipresent when He was born as a baby to Mary. Confined to flesh and bones in order to live and dwell on planet Earth with us, He is now only able to be present in one place at a time. This provides a fuller picture of what it meant when Jesus said that "God so loved the world that He gave His only begotten son."

Jesus promised that the Holy Spirit would be exactly the same as having Himself with them because the Holy Spirit would speak to them with the same wisdom, truth and insight that He had brought to them through all the days He had been with them.

The "One through whom all nations of the Earth will be blessed," had come. Jesus of Nazareth, the baby born to Mary in Bethlehem, lived His short thirty-three-and-a-half-year life in a geographic area about half the size of Nova Scotia in Canada. It is just larger than the state of New Hampshire in the United States and slightly greater in size than the country of Wales in the United Kingdom. However, the impact of His life is still reverberating all over the world.

What is it about this one life, and the way He died, that has captivated the world from that day until now? Estimates range between three hundred thousand and two million crucifixions took place during the five-hundred-year period that this method of execution was used. Crucifixion was finally abolished in the fourth century A.D. It had been mostly reserved for slaves or criminals and was never used on Roman citizens.

Why is this one particular crucifixion still being talked about today? Libraries and bookshelves have multiple volumes speaking about Jesus' birth, life and death. Music has been written about Him for centuries. A most famous composition is Handel's *Hallelujah Chorus*, where it is common practice for people to stand each time it is performed in honor of the One about whom it is written.

Sermons about this Savior are preached by the thousands each week around the world, hoping to bring new or deeper understanding about Jesus Christ of Nazareth.

What is it about this man Jesus that attracts all this attention? We will continue to explore the answer in the pages ahead.

GOD WANTS US TO REMEMBER:

- From the fateful day in Eden, when the first parents entrusted their faith in the enemy of God by disconnecting from their faith in the Creator God, they passed a death sentence on themselves and on all of us, their descendants. There was no human remedy.

- Because God is love, and only loving, He could not bear to see His created ones die without a choice. Adam and Eve had a choice, but their descendants did not. We were born in this condition. We inherited the human condition before we ever took our first breath.

- Through Jesus, God has restored the possibility for each one to have a personal choice for themselves. We must decide what to do with the sacrifice He provided for us through His own Son. We get to choose whether or not we want to accept it.

- Jesus transformed Himself into a man in order to be able to die. As God He could not die. Then He lived a perfect life, never making a bad or wrong choice. He never once gave in to any temptation the enemy put before Him. How unjust that He was crucified for sins He Himself never even committed.

- When He rose again, He offered His death and perfect life to anyone who would like to move away from the path that leads to death and transfer to the path that leads to eternal life.

13

HAVE I GOT NEWS FOR YOU!

The Book of Acts, the next book in the Bible after learning about Jesus, begins with these words: "During the forty days after He suffered and died, He appeared to the apostles from time to time, and He proved to them in many ways that He was actually alive. And He talked to them about the Kingdom of God." Acts 1:2, 3

On the last day He was with His disciples, they were all standing together on the Mount of Olives near Jerusalem. He told them that only His Father knew when He would return and that they should wait in Jerusalem until the Holy Spirit, whom He had promised, would come to them. With those final instructions, He suddenly was lifted off the earth right before their eyes and began to ascend upward into the sky above them. No doubt they stretched their necks and squinted their eyes as they kept gazing upward for one last glimpse of this One who had been their Friend, Mentor and Teacher for over three years.

Imagine their startled surprise when they suddenly noticed two angels standing nearby, who addressed them by asking, "Why are you standing here staring into Heaven? Jesus has been taken from you into heaven, but someday He will return from heaven in the same way you saw Him go!" Acts 1:11

Even with that promise, along with the fact that Jesus had assured them He would come back, I can only guess they experienced deep emptiness and grief without Him in their company. They went back to Jerusalem as instructed, waiting to see what would happen next.

While they waited, they decided it would be appropriate to choose someone to replace the disciple Judas, who had taken his own life due to the overwhelming guilt of betraying Jesus that final night in Gethsemane. After praying together, they chose a man named Matthias to join the ranks of the inner circle of disciples.

Jesus specifically called the twelve disciples to be chosen apprentices of His and also referred to them as apostles. The difference between the two titles is that "disciple" refers to anyone who desires to be mentored by Jesus. They seek a personal relationship with Him and desire to follow His teachings and lifestyle. "Apostle" is a word relating to a disciple or follower of Jesus who has been given a specific task or objective to preach the message about Jesus to the world. The twelve closest friends of Jesus would fit both categories, disciples and apostles.

Ten days after Jesus ascended to Heaven, many of these followers, along with the twelve apostles, were gathered in an upper room in Jerusalem, waiting and praying together. Suddenly, they were all startled as the room was filled with a sound like a mighty windstorm, loud enough to be heard well outside the room itself. Following that, small images that looked like tongues of fire appeared and then settled on each one gathered there. Those tongues of fire were symbols representing the Holy Spirit coming to them, just as Jesus had promised them.

There were people from many nations in Jerusalem at that time to honor and participate in the Hebrew celebration called the day of Pentecost. The noise of the wind was loud enough to attract their attention, so they ran to the room where the sound was coming from.

What happened next was rather mind-boggling. The people on whom these tongues of fire appeared suddenly began to speak in the languages of other nationalities, none of which they had spoken previously. The people visiting Jerusalem that day represented no less than at least twelve to fifteen different languages. Each one heard someone speak to them in their own native tongue.

And what did they talk about? We are told, "They were completely amazed. 'How can this be?' they exclaimed. 'These people are all from Galilee, and yet we hear them speaking in our own native languages! . . . And we all hear these people speaking in our own languages about the wonderful things God has done.'" Acts 2:7-11.

The Holy Spirit had come, and when He arrived, miraculous things began to happen. He came so the personal presence of God on Earth would continue even though Jesus had now returned to Heaven. The first activity He engaged in was sharing the truth about God to people who had never heard such things before. There was no chance of missing the message they were hearing due to a language barrier. God wanted the good news of what Jesus had accomplished to be spread far and wide, to all nations and peoples of the earth. The good news needed to be shared.

Then Peter, the disciple who had been so frightened that he denied knowing Jesus, stood up to preach to the crowd. Things had really changed for Peter. Now, he was anything but afraid to be known as a friend and disciple of Jesus. You can read his sermon in Acts chapter 2, where he pulled no punches and told the people that Jesus had come here from Heaven, had been endorsed by God, and was able to do miraculous signs and wonders. Peter went on to say that Jesus was accused and convicted by the leadership of Israel, some of the very people in the listening crowd, and carried out by the Romans who crucified Him.

Peter was very direct. He said, "with the help of the Gentiles, you nailed Him to a cross and killed Him." He then made an appeal at the end of His sermon urging people to believe in and follow Jesus. The result was astounding. Three thousand people believed what Peter had said and were baptized that very day. This was the beginning of the Christian Church. These newly baptized believers joined with those who had already expressed their belief in Jesus. The community of those who wanted to follow Jesus grew like a wildfire in a dried-out field on a windy day. There was no stopping the widening surge of excitement as the news about Jesus was shared by so many.

The book of Acts, or more formally, "The Acts of the Apostles," is a record of a few of the highlights through the first thirty years of the Christian church. The period of history covered is from approximately 33 to 60 A.D.

We are also given a snapshot of how the new believers related to each other. They would meet daily to pray together and learn about Jesus. They sold their lands and possessions to have money to promote the teachings and work of the apostles. They continued to invite people to join them, and the Christ-following community exploded in growth.

Also, there are miracle stories. One day, as Peter and John went to the temple to pray, they noticed a lame man who often sat there begging. They went over to him with more than he was expecting. Thinking they were going to give him money, imagine his joy when Peter said, "I don't have any silver or gold for you. But I'll give you what I have. In the name of Jesus Christ of Nazareth, get up and walk" Acts 3:6 The lame man did exactly that, and it says he was leaping and shouting, praising God all the way into the temple.

The disciples performed many miracles, even raising people from the dead just as Jesus had done. Jesus had told them that they would do miracles in His name, and many were witnesses to the fulfillment of those words.

One day, Peter was arrested and put in prison for preaching, fully believing he would be martyred for his faith. The night before he was to be put on trial, an angel came, opened the prison doors, released the shackles that bound him and led him out into the fresh air. He was free! Peter's work for God was not yet finished.

Sadly, we learn about Stephen, the first martyr executed for his faith in Jesus. Countless millions have died since then, simply because they saw the blessing that Jesus was to them personally, as well as to the world at large, and would not budge from their belief in Him. What makes one want to kill another for their religious faith? We can be sure it is a vindictiveness motivated only by the enemy whose vile hatred of God extends that anger and hatred toward anyone who serves God. What makes one willing to die rather than give up their belief in another person? We can be sure it is a conviction motivated only by the Spirit of God Himself.

Through a dream Peter had, it became clear to the disciples that the message of Jesus was to go to all nations, all people, all nationalities. That good news about Jesus was to go to everyone. Hebrew, Gentile, slaves, free, men, women and children. The followers of Jesus were not to be exclusive in any way. No doubt it was more comfortable to just work among their own people, but Peter's dream made it clear that they were to move out of Jerusalem to preach to everyone, everywhere.

This new perspective was underscored within the same hour after Peter awoke from his dream. There was a knock on the door by two servants of a Roman army officer named Cornelius. He had sent them to invite Peter to come and share his message about Jesus with him. This was taken as evidence to the believers that they needed to expand their mission.

One of the men who personally witnessed the martyrdom of the disciple Stephen was a hard-nosed, bully of a man, whose name was Saul. He had a very vengeful mindset, determined that his work and life calling would be to uproot and destroy people who believed in Jesus wherever he might find them. It became his life purpose. He is described as "uttering threats with every breath and was eager to kill the Lord's followers." Acts 9:1

Saul's mission knew no boundaries as one day he took a group of supporters to Damascus, approximately one hundred and fifty miles away. While on the journey, just as he was nearing the city, Saul was stunned by an extremely bright light that shone around him from the sky above, and he fell to the ground.

He heard a voice asking, "Saul! Saul! Why are you persecuting Me?"

Disoriented and trembling, he found his voice and asked, "Who are you, lord?"

"I am Jesus, the one you are persecuting. Now get up and go into the city and you will be told what you must do." Acts 9:4-6.

The result of this story is that Saul became a converted believer in Jesus. He spent much time in seclusion for the next couple of years, learning about Jesus and what His coming to this Earth had accomplished for those who live here.

Asking for the guidance of the Holy Spirit, He too became an apostle of Jesus, which he accepted as a direct calling from Jesus Himself that day when he was blinded on the road. Saul's life was forever changed. Even his name was changed by God and he would forever after be known as Paul the Apostle. The rest of the book of Acts focuses on a few of the adventures Paul had as he took the calling of God to heart. He traveled far and wide in Southern Europe and Western Asia, preaching and teaching the Good News about Jesus.

In the localities where he visited, he would establish a church group of new believers and then move on to the next place in order to repeat his mission there. Almost half of the books in the New Testament were written by Paul, of which most are letters of counsel and teaching that he wrote back to those churches after he was gone, emphasizing for them the things he really wanted them to remember.

The Gospel books tell us the story of Jesus' life. Paul's writings explain the things we are to apply to our lives about Jesus, explaining to us the very clearest understanding of how Jesus is precisely the One promised to Adam and Eve way back at the beginning. Along with the letters he wrote to the churches, he also wrote letters to personal friends such as Timothy, Titus and Philemon (Phy-lee-mon). Through Paul's writings, we are left with the best understanding of how Jesus' life, death and resurrection provide the foundation for the restoration God is planning for all of us.

After several years of travel and ministry, Paul went back to Jerusalem and was arrested by those who were threatened by the quick spread of the good news about Jesus. He stood before Roman governors who, like Pilate many years earlier with Jesus, did not want to have to make any decisions about Him. Also, like Jesus before His accusers, they could find no fault in Paul for the beliefs he was teaching. These governors were not exactly sure how to handle the charges brought against him. Finally, Paul said he wanted to appeal his case directly to Caesar. Thankful and relieved that they would not have to deal with it any longer, they assured him he would be safely taken to Rome and would be able to present his case there.

The journey to Rome was by ship. About two weeks into the trip, a storm came up that broke the ship completely apart. All two hundred and seventy-six passengers survived and got safely to shore. They had to wait there for a new ship to arrive and for the weather to settle making it safe to travel again.

When Paul arrived in Rome he was placed under arrest as they awaited charges and witnesses from Judea, or from anywhere else for that matter. Being in prison did not deter Paul as he used every opportunity he could find to tell anyone who would listen about Jesus and how belief in Him would change everything for them.

Paul remained in Rome until he died. The Bible does not record the death of Paul, we only know of it through the words and stories of the traditional records of the day. It is believed he was beheaded sometime between 64-68 A.D. and was over sixty years of age at the time of his death.

While Paul was the most prolific writer of the twenty-seven books of the New Testament, there are a few others. The books of Matthew, Mark, Luke, John and Acts are the only books that cover any record of history. The twenty-two remaining books are full of theological explanation of why Jesus matters, letters, books of counsel, and finally the prophetic book of Revelation, the last book of the whole Bible. The book of Revelation was written by the disciple John, who also wrote the gospel of John, and is believed to have been written in approximately 95 A.D. John also wrote three short letters which can be found in the Bible, just before the Book of Revelation.

It is clear from Paul's writings that his burden was to enlighten the world about Jesus. At one point, he simply said he did not want to preach or talk about anything else, just "Jesus, and Him crucified." His life purpose was to help people see the truth of who Jesus was, why His death was significant, and most of all, the crowning fact of His resurrection, which guaranteed that He was able to overcome the penalty of death that we all face.

The Book of Revelation is full of symbols, visions, beasts and angels. When understood clearly, it provides beautiful insights into the picture of Jesus Christ who conquered the enemy of God and the plague of death. The last chapters of the book, so therefore the last chapters of the Bible itself, spell out for us exactly how God is going to complete the whole restoration plan and what it is going to look like when it is complete. It is all incredibly exciting.

GOD WANTS US TO REMEMBER:

- Even though Jesus returned to Heaven, He did not leave His people to be on their own. Jesus promised the Holy Spirit would come, and since He has the divine ability to be omnipresent, He is able to be a comfort and heavenly companion for any person who seeks His guidance. And, He said the Holy Spirit's presence would be just like having Jesus Himself there with them. Through the Holy Spirit we have the presence of Jesus with us every day until He comes back again.

- Reading the four gospel accounts of Jesus coming to bless all families of the earth provides all the details and facts that we know of His life, death and resurrection. The good news of His work on our behalf needs to be told to all people around the world. This work began ten days after Jesus returned to Heaven and continues to this day.

- The people who believed in Jesus quickly formed a community that would be supportive and strengthening to each one of them as they grew, studied and prayed together. This was the beginning of the Christian church. There is always strength in numbers.

- God Himself directed and blessed the work of the church. This work is His method for sharing His very good news about restoring His original plan for all those who choose to take advantage of the opportunity.

The only difference between the saint and the sinner is that every saint has a past and every sinner has a future.

OSCAR WILDE

We are not sinners because we sin. We sin because we are sinners.

R. C. SPROUL

I have come not to call those who think they are righteous, but those who know they are sinners and need to repent.

JESUS

14

BEING A SINNER IS SIMPLY A FACT

We have been following the historical outline the Bible proclaims, but before we look at the final events that tie a bow on it all, let's probe a little deeper into a few of the major themes of the Bible which demonstrate that it is more than just a story.

It is said that we can't change or heal what we do not acknowledge. In other words, accountability regarding the truth is really the beginning of change.

I must admit that I'm in need of a lifestyle change if I want to be healthier. I must acknowledge the poor choices I have made, or the harsh words I have spoken if I want to heal a relationship. I must recognize my addiction before I can begin to live in the freedom of sobriety. Acknowledgement is the first step toward healing.

The word "sinner" has a bad connotation. Who wants to step up to the microphone and acknowledge that. "Hi, I'm Bill, and I'm a sinner." However, I want to remind you that sin is a word that describes a condition. It's not necessarily a dirty word. Cancer, Mental Health, Hepatitis, and Parkinson's are all words to describe a condition. We don't judge any person who has any one of those conditions just because they have it. Calling a person a sinner is no more judgmental than telling them that they have poor eyesight. Facts are facts.

"Sin" is a word that accurately describes the human condition we are born into through the human lineage that can trace itself all the way back to Adam and Eve. Unfortunately, innocent babies are born into this predicament when they have done absolutely nothing wrong. The condition is so debilitating it is actually called a curse in the Bible. While "curse" is an ominous word, the intent is not dark, supernatural or sinister. It simply means the human condition we are born into is terminal unless there is some act of deliverance.

This sinful predicament is the root cause of all the destructive acts that people do and the hurtful words people say that cause the grief and pain of broken relationships. The list of sinful acts in the Bible is much longer but includes things such as immorality, idolatry, strife, jealousy, gossip, outbursts of anger, envy and drunkenness. We tend to focus on the acts that come from a sinful heart, and call that sin, rather than on the fact that it is the sinful heart that produces the sinful actions.

Adam and Eve immediately hid from God after they disobeyed. Who told them they needed to do that? When He came for His end-of-the-day visit with them, they were afraid of Him for the first time ever. They blamed others for their actions. The sinful condition was on display immediately after they switched their trust and loyalty from God to the enemy of God.

The first son they conceived murdered his younger brother. Centuries later, God noticed that the hearts of men were continually evil. It has never improved since those days, even until now. Planet Earth has not become a better place to live. Chaos continuously increases. It becomes more violent, divided, diseased and polluted with each passing year.

And sadly, it is universal. Are you sinless? Do you know any sinless persons? Have you ever heard of a sinless person? Is there anyone on the planet who has never thought a selfish or revengeful thought? Never said a word they would like to take back? Never acted in a way that hurt others? Children naturally begin to exhibit selfish behavior and want their way, right now. That's because we arrive in this condition. It does not take long before we exhibit a tendency or bent toward wrongdoing and the focus on self. It is the natural point of reference that our hearts orbit around because we are born with it already embedded into our spiritual DNA.

The sad news is that without intervention there is no escape, and we are all doomed to die because of it. God clearly warned our first parents because He did not want His created beings to ever experience death. Sin is a condition that no man, woman, scientist, doctor, or philosopher has a remedy for. No wise person, parent, spouse or specialist carries the antidote. We need help from a source other than someone who is born into the same condition we are born into.

Are you putting the pieces together? This is the "Good News" of Jesus coming to us. This is the news the angels sang about the night Jesus was born. This is the good news the apostles began to teach and tell the world after Jesus went back to Heaven. This is the motivating message of the Christian church today.

The Holy One born to Mary brought the remedy with Him. Because of Him, there is a reason to hope again. He has brought the solution for our curse, our dilemma. Only He could bring it.

The conception and birth of Jesus is miraculously different from ours, which is exactly what we need. He was born of a woman, as an infant, just like us and yet not like us. When the angel came to announce to Mary that the Holy Spirit would come to her, He added that the child she would conceive would be holy and would be called the Son of God.

This child would be holy! That means without sin, set apart for a divine purpose. No human male can conceive a holy child. Mary was simply the chosen vessel who would supply the womb that would allow God the Son to be born as a human. God had formulated a perfect plan and was committed to do His supernatural work so that we could be restored. The science and procedure of how it all took place is beyond our reasoning ability. It's a very deep and mysterious topic, but we must ask ourselves, "The Bible declares it, what if it's true?"

Accepting the reality that we are in need is the first step toward finding the remedy for sin. We cannot change what we do not acknowledge. Just as Abraham Lincoln's dog does not have five legs simply because we call the tail a leg, saying we are not sinful does not make us not sinful. Acknowledging we are sinners is not the worst thing. The worst thing would be if we acknowledged we were sinners but could find no solution to the condition.

Remember how the events unfolded. After the angel told Mary she would give birth to a Holy Child, he also went to visit her fiancé in a dream and assured him that the child in Mary was different, and not to be afraid to take her as his wife. He added that this child would be the promised Savior of the world, able to "save his people from their sins."

Did you catch that? He will save His people from their sins.

There have been many wise philosophers, spiritual gurus and teachers through the centuries. They have offered insight and wisdom on any topic one can imagine. They have spoken truthful sayings and provided amazing perspectives. They have spawned denominations and faith systems. They have accumulated followers by the millions, maybe billions. Wars have been fought in the name of religion because people are defending the beliefs of a spiritual leader somewhere.

People have gone on long retreats, sought wise men and women for advice and direction. Others have lived in solitude for years. Some have tortured themselves and put themselves through requirements that have been painful and harsh because some teacher has told them this is what must be done. All in the search of meaningful answers for the deep questions of life.

However, search as one might, not one, ever, has made the claim to be able to save people from their sins, except Jesus. Only Jesus Christ of Nazareth has dared to make that claim and promise.

While Jesus was here, He had many friends. He spent much time in solitude doing His spiritual work and praying to His Father, but He was also a social being and was often found enjoying the company of others. One time, He went to Jericho in search of a man who was very unpopular. Zacchaeus (Zack-ee-us) was Jewish but collected taxes from his own people to give to the Romans. He had very few friends and was resented by everyone else.

Zacchaeus was short in stature but wanted to see Jesus, so he climbed a tree to observe Him from there when He passed by. Jesus knew he was there, so He stopped to look up into his face. Jesus asked Zacchaeus to come down because He wanted to go home with him for lunch! The people were shocked that Jesus would spend time with such a "notorious sinner," but no one was more shocked than Zacchaeus himself.

Trembling with excitement, He scrambled down from the tree and grinning like a parade marshal led the way for Jesus to follow him to his house. We don't know all they talked about, but after spending time with Jesus, Zacchaeus announced that he was going to give half his wealth to the poor and pay back all those he had cheated, multiplying his payment by four.

Jesus approved of Zacchaeus' response and said he was a true follower and that this is why He came to Earth, to "seek and save those who are lost." Jesus knew we were sinners. That didn't concern Him. He came to find anyone in this condition who wanted to be found. Acknowledging they were sinners was the path to forgiveness and healing.

There was a time in my life when my spiritual courage was fragile. I demonstrated my sinful nature as I made choices that had been destructive to my family and many friends. I was in search of spiritual assurance and health once again, wanting to know for sure that God loved me. I was visiting with a good friend, and we were talking about the condition of the human heart. He asked me a life changing question.

He invited me to read the verses in the Bible found in Romans chapter 5, verses 6 through 10. He asked me to pick out the four conditions of the human heart listed in those verses that Jesus came to die for. I found them within just a few moments.

The text says that Jesus came and died for us while we were (1) utterly helpless, (2) ungodly, (3) sinners, and (4) enemies. "While we were" these things. These words sum up the sinful condition of the human heart, handed down to us from Adam and Eve.

Then my friend posed a question that changed everything for me. He asked, "Bill, if these are the four conditions that Jesus died for, do you qualify?" With peace flooding my heart, I realized that simply admitting I was one or all those things qualified me for His gift of restoration.

The beautiful truth about Jesus is that He is just fine with our admission of the fact we are sinners. He can do nothing for those who are unable or unwilling to acknowledge they have a need. He cannot help those who believe they are already righteous and condescendingly look down on those they would judge to be the "scum," of life. These people don't believe they need any help. The good news is that He can do everything for those who admit they qualify for His grace and desire to be near Him. He even loves to go home to spend time with them.

What if it's true that Jesus came to be with you simply because you acknowledge that you qualify?

BIBLE TEXTS THAT DECLARE THIS THEME:

- For everyone has sinned; we all fall short of God's glorious standard. Romans 3:23

- When Adam sinned, sin entered the world. Adam's sin brought death, so death spread to everyone, for everyone sinned. Romans 5:12

- The human heart is the most deceitful of all things, and desperately wicked. Who really knows how bad it is? Jeremiah 17:9

- Who can say, 'I have cleansed my heart; I am pure and free from sin?' Proverbs 20:9

- If we claim we have no sin, we are only fooling ourselves and not living in the truth. 1 John 1:8

- The angel to Mary, "The baby to be born will be holy, and he will be called the Son of God." Luke 1:35

- The angel to Joseph, "Do not be afraid to take Mary as your wife. For the child within her was conceived by the Holy Spirit. And she will have a son, and you are to name him Jesus, for he will save his people from their sins." Matthew 1:20, 21.

- Jesus said to Zacchaeus, "Salvation has come to this home today, for this man has shown himself to be a true son of Abraham. For the Son of Man came to seek and save those who are lost." Luke 19:9, 10

- Jeshua's clothing was filthy as he stood there before the angel. So the angel said to the others standing there, 'Take off his filthy clothes.' And turning to Jeshua he said, 'See I have taken away your sins, and now I am giving you these fine new clothes.' Zechariah 3:3, 4

- When we were utterly helpless, Christ came at just the right time and died for us sinners. . . . God showed his great love for us by sending Christ to die for us while we were still sinners. Romans 5:6 & 8

- But if we confess our sins to him, he is faithful and just to forgive us our sins and to cleanse us from all wickedness. 1 John 1:9

- "'Come now, let's settle this,' says the LORD. 'Though your sins are like scarlet, I will make them white as snow. Though they are red like crimson, I will make them as white as wool.'" Isaiah 1:18

Some people are so afraid to die that they never begin to live.

HENRY VAN DYKE

We live and die; Christ died and lived!

JOHN STOTT

Jesus' death wasn't to free us from dying, but to free us from the fear of death.

ERWIN MCMANUS

15

YOU ARE SURE TO DIE

When God warned Adam and Eve not to eat of the fruit of the tree of the knowledge of good and evil, He added, "If you eat its fruit, you are sure to die."

When the serpent/enemy talked with Eve and she told him that God had warned that death would be the consequence of eating the fruit, he scoffingly said, "You won't die." He added that God was unfair, withholding information from her and didn't want her to know that instead of dying, the fruit would actually make her wise. That was a whole new perspective. Eve had a decision to make! They couldn't both be right. Which one was lying? Was God telling the truth, or was the serpent telling the truth? Would she in fact die, or would she become wise?

Tragically she decided the enemy was correct, ate the fruit, and all too soon came to realize that he was the one who had been lying. Can you imagine the level of regret she experienced? Even now, centuries later, we continue to experience the grief that comes along with death. We have been to funerals. We have possibly been present or sat by a bedside as someone we love is looking death straight in the eye. Maybe even held someone's hand as they passed away.

Friends and loved ones of ours are no longer with us. It is estimated that around the world more than one hundred and seventy thousand people die every day. That's over seven thousand every hour, one hundred and nineteen every minute. The proof is evident! God was indeed right when He said, "You are sure to die."

What does it really mean to die? We now get to the heart of the matter as to why Jesus came from Heaven to live among us, die on the cross and be resurrected again. In the next couple of chapters, we will explore a deeper picture of why Jesus Christ (or Messiah) deeply impacts each one of us regarding the reality of death.

There are a variety of beliefs about death. Some are terrified of the whole topic, afraid to even talk about it, except maybe at Hallowe'en. It is not a casual topic, usually brought up only when circumstances force us to.

Many accept it to merely be a transition to a new existence outside of the bodies we live in while on Earth. Thus, a common belief is that death means we transfer straight to Heaven where we take up residence with God, angels, and those we love who died and went there before us. Upon our death we join them in the enjoyment of Heaven as well as observing the ongoing life of loved ones left behind. Others are convinced that at death, we change from the bodies we live in now and come back to dwell on the earth in some other form, maybe even that of an animal or creature. Many do not give it much thought at all and are just content to discover what happens when the time comes.

Genesis tells us that when Adam was created, God formed His body from the dust of the earth. What a miracle! And there on the ground lay the first man, with all organs and systems in place. Silent, still, unmoving, and unaware of his surroundings.

Think of it. For everything else God created He spoke it into existence. When it came to mankind, God knelt on the ground, lovingly formed the first human body with His hands, then bent over and gently breathed life into Adam's nostrils. The result? "The man BECAME a living person." (Genesis 2:7) Some versions say, "living soul." Adam was not already a living soul in some other form before he came to live in the body God had just formed. The Bible says nothing about that.

The man "became a living soul" at the exact moment the breath of life flowed into the body He had created with His hands.

Death was never part of the original plan. It was God's design that mankind would live forever. God is the only One who never dies, and that was what He had in mind for those He created in His image. There was another tree in the Garden, called the Tree of Life. Adam and Eve were counseled to eat from this tree as it was the source of immortal life for them. It was not that the fruit of that tree was supernatural or life-giving on its own, but each time they ate that fruit, it was a display of continual trust in the Creator God for life. As long as they ate the fruit of that tree they would never die.

When He warned them not to eat from the Tree of the Knowledge of Good and Evil, He made it clear that if they did in fact eat its fruit, that would be the day death would become part of their existence. They were duped by the serpent who said, "You will not die." When they turned away from the Creator of life and ate the forbidden fruit, they were not allowed to remain in the garden, forfeiting their access to the Tree of Life.

The Biblical description of death is that when a person dies, the reverse of the original creation process happens. The body and the breath simply separate again. You've heard the statement, "Dust to dust." The body deteriorates and returns to dust and the life-giving source, the breath of life, returns to God. The spirit is the breath of life that God breathed into the man at the time of creation. That life force simply returns to God, the source of all life.

Computers provide a great illustration for this mysterious topic. For a computer to work, at least three components are necessary. It needs hardware, which includes items such as the box the computer comes in, a screen, hard drive and keyboard. However, the hardware is useless all by itself.

For a computer to do its amazing work it also needs software, the information that works in conjunction with the hardware to run the programs, make calculations, as well as share and store data. It is also true that the software by itself is useless without the hardware. The two must be joined together to bring about the desired results.

Even that is not enough. Finally, the computer of course needs electricity to bring all the components to life.

The body God formed from the dust of the earth is like the hardware. The skeleton and organs of the man were present, but unable to do anything. The breath of life He breathed into the man is a great metaphor for the electricity that runs the computer. The living soul that mankind became is similar to the software package that runs it all and brings about the desired result.

The living soul makes decisions about everything in life. When to eat, exercise, love, and work. It's the part of us that displays attitude, anger, passion and personality. It is here that we make decisions regarding friends, relationships, God, morality, as well as all things spiritual.

As with computers, if the software is backed up, it matters not if the hardware gets destroyed. We can beat the box, smash the hard drive, even burn the keyboard, and the stored software will still run again, smoothly, in a new computer.

The software, or the soul, is not able to respond to any event in life on its own. It needs the body and the breath of life from God to accomplish anything.

When God said they would die if they ate the fruit, He was letting them know that they would die a permanent death. Death meant a total separation from life because that is logically what happens when we turn away from the One who gave us life in the first place. He was pleading with them to stay away from that tree and avoid it at all cost. It was a test of their loyalty to Him and the acknowledgement that they were dependent on Him for eternal life.

When they ate the fruit, they sentenced themselves to death, yet in God's mercy, they did not die instantly. Instead, He promised that a Savior would come who would crush the enemy whose temptation brought on the death sentence. However, conquering the one who seduced them into the condition of death would be of no value unless He also conquered the punishment, death itself. We have already seen that Jesus claimed to be that Savior, and because of Him, death does not have to be permanent. Because Jesus died and was resurrected from the dead, we now have the possibility to be resurrected to eternal life as well.

The Bible speaks of only two individuals, Enoch and Elijah, who went to Heaven without ever dying, but that is not the norm. The law of the tombstone says, "There is one for each of us," and it is unrelenting.

But here is what some miss. There are two types of death. The Bible calls them the first death and the second death. The penalty for sin is permanent death. Death we never come back from. Jesus used the word, "perish" when He spoke with Nicodemus in John 3:16

However, the Bible also calls death a sleep. We all know that when we are in a deep sleep, time goes by, and life goes on around us that we know nothing about. Nevertheless, sleep is something we eventually wake up from.

So, which is it? Permanent perishing, or a temporary sleep?

In the Old Testament there are thirty-six references to kings of Israel, stating when they reigned, what they accomplished, and a little bit about their lives. Without fail for each one, the record of their lives ends with the same statement: ". . . and they slept with their fathers and were buried with their fathers."

Numerous verses from Scripture describe death in this way.

How fascinating then that we read about Jesus resurrecting people from the dead while He was here with us. When He spoke about death He regularly referred to death as a sleep.

Jairus (Jy-russ) was a leader of a local synagogue who came to Jesus, pleading passionately with Him to come to his house because his twelve-year-old daughter was dying. Jesus said He would go and started moving through the crowd with Jairus. He was delayed by people pressing in around Him making His progress very slow. Finally, a messenger came and reported to Jairus' that his daughter had already died so there was no need to trouble Jesus any further.

Jesus heard them talking and said, "Don't be afraid, just have faith," and kept going toward Jairus' home. He knew she had died but didn't want that to be the end of the story.

When He arrived, He found a crowd of people weeping and crying. He asked, "Why all this commotion and weeping? She isn't dead; she's only asleep." They scoffed at Him, but He went on into the room where she was lying, took her by the hand and raised her back to life by saying "Little girl, get up!" He was the only one able to awaken her from this sleep.

When Lazarus, one of His close friends, was dying, his sisters sent word to Jesus, thinking He would come immediately to heal Lazarus. Jesus told His disciples that Lazarus' sickness would not end in death, and He stayed there two more days. He then said to His disciples, "Lazarus has gone to sleep, but I'm going to go wake him up."

The disciples commented on how sleep would be good for Lazarus and that he would get well now, but Jesus told them that when He said that Lazarus was asleep, He in fact meant that Lazarus had died.

Many are shocked to discover that, contrary to popular belief, the Bible does not tell us we go to Heaven immediately when we die. The Bible does not tell us that those who pass away are then reunited with friends and loved ones, recording heavenly birthdays, or watching us who are left behind as we live out our lives here. The Bible does tell us that when death happens, we sleep, and we don't know anything about what is happening back here. We absolutely do eventually transfer to Heaven, just not at the moment of death. We will address this more fully in a few pages.

In our grief we want to think that our loved ones have not gone to a lonely grave, but instead to a better place, so Heaven is the best possible option. Let's pause and think about that. If it were true that when we take our last breath in our human body on Earth, then take the next breath in the beauty and bliss of Heaven, it would be God that was lying back in the garden and the enemy was telling the truth when he told Eve she wouldn't really die! Going to Heaven at the time of death means we just keep living somewhere else.

The true definition of death is that it is the end of life. It is the consequence of turning away from the source of life and giving our loyalty to the enemy. It is perishing, not the process of transference from one location to another.

It is important to address a question that may be coming up for some. This topic deserves to be explored in much greater detail with other, deeper resources, but I do not want to simply step over or ignore it.

It is not uncommon to hear stories about loved ones who pass away and then come back to visit friends or family members from time to time. They have been seen, even conversed with. How do we reconcile that the Bible says that all who have died are asleep in death when there seems to be anecdotal evidence to the contrary?

Since the enemy's lie to Eve was in essence "You will not die even though God said you would," we can be sure that he will do his best to strengthen that lie in any way he can. Having loved ones appear to us after they have died suggests strong evidence that he was in fact telling us the truth.

Hollywood movies and television do their part in promoting this topic, writing storylines that make it seem obvious that our dead friends remain active and are not far away.

The Bible is consistent about death and addresses this issue when it informs us about something called "Familiar Spirits." This term refers to supernatural entities impersonating our loved ones, but they are not our actual loved ones. They are familiar, but they are not who we are led to believe they are. They look and talk just like those we know, all in the attempt to have us continue to believe the lie that we don't really die. The Bible clearly addresses the practices of witchcraft, sorcery, speaking with familiar spirits, and the like, and implores us to avoid these things entirely because it is all the work of God's enemy.

I remember an incident when an elderly church member asked me as her pastor to go with her to visit a friend whose husband had recently passed away. When we arrived, we found this eighty-something lady in deep grief, hardly able to talk without tearing up or sobbing. She described the details of his death, her subsequent loss, and her ensuing loneliness. She was somewhat paralyzed in her grief and could not talk about anything else.

Then she added, "He came to visit me, twice. Once in my bedroom in the night, and then another time standing right there by the wood heater. When he came to my bedroom he just stood by the bed and never said anything. When he came here to the living room he just stood and stared at me, so I finally asked him, 'Is there something you want?' With that, he just disappeared."

I looked at my friend, wondering, "Do I tell her that I don't believe it was really her husband?" I didn't want to in some way increase her grief by telling her what I really believed. I was very unsure about what to do.

After a few moments of silence she asked, "You do believe it was my husband, don't you?"

I could not ignore that direct question, so with a silent prayer I responded with, "Well, no, I do not believe it was your husband. I believe it was the enemy of God trying to play a trick on you by having something appear to you that looked exactly like your husband, but it was not actually him." I explained to her how the Bible tells us that "the living at least know they will die, but the dead know nothing." Ecclesiastes 9:5 I explained that the Bible speaks of death being a temporary sleep, and that our loved ones do not go to Heaven when they die. While simply sound asleep in death they are safe in the heart and mind of God as they await the moment of resurrection.

I paused, wondering if this would upset her even further. After a brief time to process it all, I was delighted when she said, "That's the best news I have heard in a long time. It's much better to know he's sleeping rather than watching me cry all the time. Can I get you something to eat?" And with that she dried her tears, got up and served us a light snack. She was lighter and brighter and thanked us profusely for our visit which had helped answer her questions.

The Bible tells us that even Jesus did not go to Heaven when He died on the cross. On the morning He was resurrected, Mary, one of His friends, in her grief went to the tomb to be near His body. Through her tears, she spoke to a man standing there whom she thought was the gardener. Suddenly she recognized Him and cried out, "Teacher!"

Jesus said to Mary, "Don't cling to me, for I have not yet ascended to the Father." Then He asked her to go find the disciples and tell them that He was going now to see His Father and that He would meet them later in Galilee. Jesus didn't go straight to Heaven when He died, and there is no Biblical teaching that says we do either.

Jesus makes this abundantly clear as we finish the story of Lazarus and his sisters. When He arrived in Bethany, sister Martha met Him first and said to Him: "Lord, if only you had been here, my brother would not have died."

'Your brother will rise again,' Jesus reminded her.

'Yes,' Martha said, 'he will rise when everyone else rises, on the last day.'

Jesus told her, 'I am the resurrection and the life. Anyone who believes in me will live, even after dying. Everyone who lives in me and believes in me will never ever die.' John 11:21-26

Herein lies the difference. Finally, there is hope beyond the grave. Until now, all of humanity faced the inevitability of permanent death. Because of Jesus, and ONLY because of Jesus, the penalty of death has been amended to now include another option. Just as no one has ever said they were able to forgive sin, neither has there been one who has offered life beyond the grave. In fact, eternal life beyond the grave. Only Jesus has made those claims. He offers both forgiveness of the sinful human condition and hope for eternal life.

This is why through Him, all the nations of the world would be blessed. Without Jesus, death would still be the inevitable, permanent result of our sinful condition. Because of Jesus, the gift of immortality is now a promised gift within reach once again for anyone who believes that Jesus is that promised Savior.

Earlier I referred to two types of death. One is a temporary sleep that ends in eternal life. The other is a temporary sleep that will ultimately end in a permanent death.

Jesus clearly told us how to qualify for the sleep of death that ends in eternal life when He spoke to Martha. I repeat His statement so that we don't miss it: "**I am the resurrection and the life. Anyone who believes in me will live, even after dying. Everyone who lives in me and believes in me will never ever die.**" If we believe in Jesus, we may die the death of sleep, but we will never die the permanent death. There is a resurrection coming for those who qualify for the "just sleeping" list.

The death of sleep until the moment of resurrection at the return of Jesus is referred to as the first death. The death that lasts forever is referred to as the second death. More will be said on this in the pages ahead.

Jesus is the central figure of the Bible, and this topic is the centerpiece of the Good News about why Jesus came to Earth. Finally, once and for all the penalty and curse of death has been lifted, and the God's supremacy over death has been guaranteed through Him. When He returns, we will finally experience the fulfillment of the promises He made about the future together with Him.

BIBLE TEXTS THAT DECLARE THIS THEME:

- "Then the LORD God formed the man from the dust of the ground. He breathed the breath of life into the man's nostrils, and the man became a living person." Genesis 2:7 Or, "Man became a living soul." (NKJV)

- "But the LORD God warned him (Adam), 'You may freely eat the fruit of every tree in the garden–except the tree of the knowledge of good and evil. If you eat its fruit, you are sure to die." Genesis 2:16, 17

- The enemy said, "You won't die! God knows that your eyes will be opened as soon as you eat it, and you will be like God." Genesis 3:4

- Paul said, speaking of God, "He who is the blessed and only Sovereign, the King of kings and Lord of lords, who alone possesses immortality." 1 Timothy 6:16 NASB

- God said to Adam, "By the sweat of your brow you will have food to eat until you return to the ground from which you were made. For you were made from dust, and to dust you will return." Genesis 3:19

- "How do you know what your life will be like tomorrow? Your life is like the morning fog—it's here a little while, and then it's gone." James 4:14

- "The dust returns to the earth as it was: and the spirit shall return unto God who gave it." Ecclesiastes 12:7

- "The living at least know that they will die, but the dead know nothing. They have no further reward." Ecclesiastes 9:5

- "Whatever you do, do well. For when you go to the grave, there will be no work or planning or knowledge or wisdom." Ecclesiastes 9:10

- "Give no regard to mediums and familiar spirits; do not seek after them, to be defiled by them: I am the LORD your God." Leviticus 19:31 NKJV

- "How frail is humanity! How short is life, how full of trouble! We blossom like a flower and then wither. Like a passing shadow, we quickly disappear." Job 14:1, 2

- Jesus to Mary on the morning of His resurrection, "Don't cling to me, for I have not yet ascended to the Father. But go find my brothers and tell them, 'I am ascending to my Father and your Father, to my God and your God." John 20:17.

- God to the prophet Daniel, "As for you, go your way until the end. You will rest, and then at the end of the days, you will rise again to receive the inheritance set aside for you." Daniel 12:13

- Paul Speaking, "As for me, my life has already been poured out as an offering to God. The time of my death is near. I have fought the good fight. I have finished the race, and I have remained faithful. And now the prize awaits me—the crown of righteousness, which the Lord, the righteous Judge, will give me on the day of his return. And the prize is not just for me but for all who eagerly look forward to his appearing." 2 Timothy 4:6-8

Jesus basically summarized the whole Bible in one of His parables when He said:

"The Kingdom of Heaven is like a farmer who planted good seed in his field. But that night as the workers slept, his enemy came and planted weeds among the wheat, then slipped away. When the crop began to grow and produce grain, the weeds also grew.

The farmer's workers went to him and said, 'Sir, the field where you planted that good seed is full of weeds! Where did they come from?'

'An enemy has done this!' the farmer exclaimed.

'Should we pull out the weeds?' they asked.

'No,' he replied, 'you'll uproot the wheat if you do. Let both grow together until the harvest. Then I will tell the harvesters to sort out the weeds, tie them into bundles, and burn them, and to put the wheat in the barn'

Later He explained the parable to His disciples like this when He added, "The Son of Man is the farmer who plants the good seed. The field is the world, and the good seed represents the people of the Kingdom. The weeds are the people who belong to the evil one. The enemy who planted the weeds among the wheat is the devil. The harvest is the end of the world, and the harvesters are the angels. Matthew 13: 24-30, 37-40

God's creation was perfect. An enemy planted evil and death into the perfect world God planned. Instead of God just uprooting the evil, in His wisdom He is leaving it all until the end of the world with the plan to deal with sin, death and restoration all at once. That is when death will cease to be part of our existence. In the meantime, we are forced to grapple with it all on a regular basis. However, we live in the hope of God's promises knowing that one day all will be perfect again.

God has no grandchildren. He only has children, so being a born-again Christian is not an automatic thing.

RICHARD BONNKE

What good does it do me if Christ was born in Bethlehem once if he is not born again in my heart through faith?

ORIGEN

When you're born again, your DNA changes. You have the ability to understand God's terms.

BILL MCCARTNEY

16

BEING BORN AGAIN IS NOT
A GOOD IDEA

Since acknowledging the reality of our inherited sinful human condition is actually a good thing, what happens after that?

Well, if eternal life is available to anyone who chooses it, the fact that the "wages of sin is death" is a moot point for anyone who takes advantage of what God has done for us through Jesus. He came to offer an exit ramp off the highway that leads to eternal death. He came to say, "I have a gift for you. You can't earn it, and you can't buy it. But you can have it for free, if you want it."

That's the challenge for us. Are we able to be humble enough to simply reach out, take His gift and accept it when we really don't deserve it?

This highlights why Jesus is the central figure of the whole Bible. The Old Testament continually points forward to Him, and the New Testament continually points back to Him. Through Jesus we all have hope, assurance and a guarantee for a restored outcome.

The most quoted text of all the Bible lays it out so simply and clearly. Speaking with Nicodemus, a religious leader in Jerusalem, Jesus said, "For God so loved the world that he gave his only begotten Son, that whosoever believeth in him should not perish, but have everlasting life." John 3:16 NKJV

The New Living Translation version of the Bible records that same text this way. "For this is how God loved the world: He gave his one and only Son, so that everyone who believes in him will not perish but have eternal life." Everyone also means anyone. The condition for access to this promise is not earning it, but simply by believing in Jesus.

Notice the two options He mentioned. Perish means to eternally die with no hope to ever live again. Eternal life means life that never experiences eternal death. We may die, (sleep for a bit), but if we have faith in Jesus, that sleep is only temporary.

As Jesus talked with Nicodemus, He spoke in language all of us would be able to easily understand. He explained to him that judgment against anyone will not be on what actions people did or did not do, but would be based on whether or not they accepted the gift offered by Jesus. They could embrace the light of truth that He brought, and live, or continue to embrace the darkness, the deceptive lies of the devil, and perish. This is the one and only option that makes the difference between eternal life or eternal death.

In the conversation with Nicodemus, Jesus went on to explain how to access this option. He said, "I tell you the truth, unless you are born again, you cannot see the Kingdom of God."

Nicodemus protested, "What do you mean? How can an old man go back into his mother's womb and be born again?"

Jesus added that being born in the human, physical way, (born of water) was the only type of life that humans can produce. But He quickly added that the Holy Spirit gives birth to spiritual life, (born of the Spirit) the life and relationship He had originally created us for. He was informing Nicodemus that without that second, spiritual birth, there was no way to ever see the eternal life offered in the Kingdom of God.

Therefore, the title of this chapter is true. Being born again is not simply a good idea, it is a critical decision that has eternal consequences! It is the one avenue to experience the only way out of the dilemma we inherited at birth. Jesus could not have said it any clearer. It's free, and it's offered to us, should we choose to accept it.

BEING BORN AGAIN IS NOT A GOOD IDEA

"Born of the Spirit" is a reference to our need to have the Holy Spirit work within our hearts and minds to nourish a spiritual life, one that we don't possess naturally at birth. Children have real questions about spiritual topics. Their unbridled curiosity can be taught about Jesus at an early age. There is no question the Holy Spirit is at work on young minds when they are invited to learn about Jesus.

When we are born again, an increased interest in the things of God awakens within us. We have a new thirst for an understanding of heavenly matters. We begin to investigate a spiritual perspective to our everyday lives. The desire to include God in our daily awareness comes alive within us, changing our priorities and perspectives.

If this all seems a bit mysterious, that is understandable. It's not easy to explain. Jesus painted a word picture to help us when He said to Nicodemus that we can see the trees moving, and the effect of the wind, but we don't see the wind itself. We don't know where it's coming from or where it's going. He explained that this is what it's like to be born of the Spirit. We don't see the Holy Spirit at work, but we certainly observe the changes in the lives of people who shift their allegiance to God.

The difference between the human mind and the born-again mind is contrasted in different ways. In the Old Testament, the prophet Ezekiel speaks about the human heart being "stony" and the spiritual heart being a heart of flesh. One is hard, the other soft and pliable.

Those who are born again and look forward to eternal life are not a special, privileged group of the exclusive or elite. Being born again is not for a select few only. It's offered freely to anyone willing to acknowledge they are sinners in need of help. It's about recognizing the reality of our condition, and then accepting the remedy offered.

God does not hide the truth from people and then judge them for not believing in Him. If there is no interest or desire to be led by the Holy Spirit and to be born again, the whole idea of God, Jesus, death and resurrection will seem completely unnecessary. The human heart does not automatically desire these things. God never uses force to

175

make His point. He simply informs, offers, and invites, then leaves the choice with us.

The Apostle Paul declared that if we are not interested in the things of God, the whole message of Jesus and His crucifixion will sound like foolishness. That is a startling statement, maybe even a wakeup call for some.

Jesus' disciple and good friend John said that everyone who met Him, accepted Him and believed in Him, were reborn, and it was to them that Jesus gave the right to become the children of God.

The same Peter who publicly denied he even knew Jesus made a very bold declaration in his sermon on the Day of Pentecost stating that there was no other name or way under Heaven in which we will be rescued and saved. To him, it was only through Jesus, or not at all.

There is a belief that "all roads get us to Heaven," and no matter what route we take we will all eventually arrive there. That is a philosophical position that is certainly attractive; however, it's not a Biblical position. The theme of the Bible centers around Jesus, the Son of God, who came to this Earth for one reason only! His one and only goal was to guarantee a path of restoration back to that which was lost.

No philosophy or grand awareness answers the significant questions of our deep spiritual need. "The Universe" does not have an intimate knowledge of our names, our hearts, nor does it offer the relationship our souls desire. "The Universe" cannot heal my human condition. A "higher power" does not provide the personal comfort we may crave in a time of loss or brokenness. Spiritual leaders, pastors, shamans and gurus may have wonderful words of wisdom and truth, even life transforming rules to live by, but they are only human like us and we need someone to offer us far more than grand ideas.

We need a Savior. We need someone able to do what we are not capable of doing for ourselves.

The obvious question then is how does one become "Born Again?" What do we need to do to make that happen?

I'm so glad you asked! It's not hard and it's very doable for anyone.

Step one is accountability. To begin, we need to recognize and acknowledge that we are born as a sinner in a condition of need. With this heritage, at best, if we are one of the lucky ones, we live a few decades and then we die. Unless we get help, this is all there is.

Step two is accepting and believing that Jesus is who He claims to be, the One who came to us to give us that help we so desperately need. He said He came to give His life as a ransom for us, and by dying in our place He removed the inevitable penalty from us. When we accept His perfect life and death as a replacement of our own less than perfect lives, we are declaring that we believe in Him.

Maybe you have heard of something called "The Sinner's Prayer." It's very simple and it summarizes everything in a few words. There is no specific prayer needed, just a simple acknowledgement of our need for Jesus. Here is an example: "Lord Jesus, I welcome you into my life. I believe that you are the Son of God and you died on the cross to save me from darkness and grant me Eternal Life. Lord Jesus, forgive me my sins and accept me into Your Kingdom. Today, I make this decision to give my life to You and live my life for you."

When the heart sincerely wants to live in relationship with Jesus that's all it takes to be born again!

Step three is to begin and then commit to the journey of building a trusting relationship with Jesus. We intentionally spend time with Him. We dig deeper in the Bible than this overview provides and seek to gain a more intimate knowledge of His desire for us. We learn to pray and discover that communication with Him becomes a rewarding habit. We continually invite Him to dwell in our hearts (minds) in order to reorient our lives around His purpose and goal for us. This is what many refer to as "giving my heart to Jesus."

That's all there is to it. Everything pivots around one very big word, surrender. That word is so difficult for the human heart to accept and respond to, but it is the ultimate step that qualifies for being "born again." It is the one thing that Eve did not do when enticed by the enemy. It is the only thing Jesus did the entire time He lived among us.

It is more than a logical, intellectual decision. There is a spiritual, heartfelt change. When we meet Jesus this way, and worship Him, He assures us that we are forgiven and on the road that leads to a guaranteed restoration. Then He says, "Follow Me. Come be an apprentice of Me."

Being Born Again is just the beginning of this journey. Now we choose to learn of Him with the goal to become like Him. We learn how to love like He loves! We learn to orient our lives around God's desires for us, not just our desires. The people in His day said nobody ever spoke like Him. They were amazed at His insights when He had never registered in their schools or learned from the teachers of the day. He was different from anyone they had ever known or listened to.

Would you like to be an apprentice of His, and learn His ways?

It's very simple, but simple is not always easy. The enemy does not want any of us to turn our loyalty away from him and put it back on the God who created us. Satan will resist and remind us of where we have failed in the past and tell us that we aren't good enough to be accepted by God. And our answer should be, "You are right, I'm not good enough, but Jesus is good enough and He is giving me His perfect, good-enough life as a gift."

We will never be able to earn God's gift, but we can reach out and accept it! If eternity means anything to us, it's the only option we have.

Jesus loves to remind us, "I know everything about you, I know you need me. That's why I came! I know you have made mistakes. I get it and I fully understand. I'm here to fix what you are not able to fix yourselves. Do you believe I am able to do that? Will you let me come into your heart and life and transform you?"

Our answer to that question determines whether or not we believe in Him. If we say yes, we are born again, and we begin the journey of what it means to live on the path that leads to eternal life rather than the path that leads to death.

This is why being born again is not just a good idea! Instead, it's absolutely crucial if we ever want to experience the restoration God has planned and receive the immortality that God wants to give us.

What If it's true? If it is, then it's not a decision we can be casual about.

A few questions remain, such as, "How will the pain and suffering of this world all end, and when is this restoration going to happen?" Let's talk about that.

BIBLE TEXTS THAT DECLARE THIS THEME:

- "For the wages of sin is death, **BUT** the free gift of God is eternal life through Christ Jesus our Lord." Romans 6:23 (Emphasis mine)

- "For God so loved the world that he gave his only begotten Son, that whosoever believeth in him should not perish, but have everlasting life." John 3:16 NKJV

- "For this is how God loved the world: He gave his one and only Son, so that everyone who believes in him will not perish but have eternal life." John 3:16

- "I assure you, no one can enter the Kingdom of God without being born of water and the Spirit. Humans can produce only human life, but the Holy Spirit gives birth to spiritual life." John 3:5, 6

- "There is no judgement against anyone who believes in him. (Jesus) But anyone who does not believe in him has already been judged for not believing in God's one and only Son. And the judgment is based on this fact: God's light came into the world, but people loved the darkness more than the light, for their actions were evil." John 3:18, 19.

- "The wind blows where it wants. Just as you can hear the wind but can't tell where it's coming from or where it's going, so you can't explain how people are born of the Spirit." John 3:8

- God speaking, "And I will give you a new heart, and I will put a new spirit in you. I will take out your stony, stubborn heart and give you a tender, responsive heart. And I will put my Spirit in you so that you will follow my decrees and be careful to obey my regulations." Ezekiel 36: 26, 27

- Peter speaking, "There is salvation in no one else! (Jesus) God has given no other name under heaven by which we must be saved." Acts 4:12.

- Paul speaking, "The message of the cross is foolish to those who are headed for destruction! But we who are being saved know it is the very power of God." 1 Corinthians 1:18

- "To all who believed him and accepted him, he gave the right to become children of God. They are reborn—not with a physical birth resulting from human passion or planning, but a birth that comes from God." John 1:12, 13

- "God saved you by his grace when you believed. And you can't take credit for this; it is a gift from God. Salvation is not a reward for the good things we have done, so none of us can boast about it." Ephesians 2:8, 9

- "For God made Christ, who never sinned, to be the offering for our sin, so that we could be made right with God through Christ" 2 Corinthians 5:21

17

WHY JESUS QUALIFIES

Who is this Jesus really? What qualifies Him to fulfill the claim that He is the One to bless all the nations of the earth? He angered the leaders of the nation of Israel when He claimed to be the Messiah, the Son of God. He is the leading character of the Bible. He presents Himself as the ultimate solution to the complicated dilemma humanity is in, but what is it that qualifies Him to be all these things to us?

We have already noticed how His birth differs from ours. He was born to a virgin, and that was accomplished because of the promise of an angel that the Holy Spirit would implant the Holy embryo within her. He would be human so He could relate to us and experience our life along with us. He would also be God so that He could do things for us that no one else is able to. This is the reason the angel was able to promise Joseph that Jesus would save people from their sins.

Then, our Savior needs to be someone who would not turn their loyalty away from God at any time and give in to the temptation of the enemy, like Eve, and Adam had done. We need someone who would completely and fully obey the words of God. TOTALLY. Without fail, at any time, even in the slightest. It had to be perfect obedience. Something that not one of us has ever been able to do.

Jesus qualifies for that too. He lived here on Earth with us for just over thirty-three years, being tempted just like we are. The Bible declares that He met those temptations without ever giving in or responding to His own desires or wants. He was only willing to do that which His Father directed Him to say or do.

Of course He was never tempted to watch inappropriate television, movies or videos, because He didn't have those temptations to deal with. He never had to deal with chatter of social media or road rage. The specific temptations He faced may be different, but the TYPES of temptations are identical.

Sin is following the automatic desire to do what I want to do in any given moment rather than seeking guidance from the One who created me. We can come up with amazing rationalization as to why our decisions are logical and acceptable. The serpent's ultimate temptation to Eve was, "just think this through for yourself and do what makes sense to you." That's the crux of the issue. Sin's temptation is to do what we want! Do what makes sense! Do what feels good! "It's your life, don't let anyone else tell you how to live it."

That's why surrender is the crux of the issue.

Jesus was no doubt tempted to get angry and react harshly when the religious leaders would continually seek to trap Him with His own words. He was probably tempted to heatedly put His disciples in their place when they kept arguing about which one of them was the greatest. He was a young man, and no doubt noticed female beauty around Him, but was never inappropriate, even in His thoughts. He experienced all the temptations of the human experience just as we do, but He didn't give in to them at any time.

No doubt there were times that He was weary to the bone. We know from experience that in those moments, we are susceptible to saying or doing things we wish we could take back. But He never did.

He spent hours in prayer and communion with His Father. He would slip away from His disciples while they slept, sometimes praying all night. As a result, whenever He was confronted with temptation, He always had the desire and the strength to choose to do what His Father would want from Him.

And, because of that, here's the most important detail that qualifies Him to be our Savior. He never, ever committed a sin. Yet He allowed them to crucify Him, submitting to the most shameful of all deaths.

As He prayed in the Garden of Gethsemane on the night before He died, He pleaded with His Father three different times that if possible, could "this cup" be taken away from Him so He would not have to drink it? He was so distraught that sweat fell from Him like great drops of blood. He was in absolute agony. Why? He was not the first or last to suffer crucifixion. It was a torturous punishment for sure, one that no one would ever want to experience, but there seemed to be something deeper going on for Jesus. What was the root of His distressed, passionate pleading?

It was this! The Bible declares, "He personally carried our sins in his body on the cross so that we can be dead to sin and live for what is right. By His wounds you were healed." 1 Peter 2:24

Do you see it? He was sinless, yet He chose to die because of our sins, and for our sins. The sins that we committed. He died for sins that He never committed. He chose to take them on Himself and own them as if they were His. That means although He never murdered anyone, He took on the same guilt as if He was a murderer. He bore the same guilt as if He was a thief. As if He was a liar, and as if He was an adulterer. He took on the guilt of a violent rebel, a pedophile, and all things lustful. Whatever sinful act one can imagine, no matter how ugly, brutal or disgusting, He took that on too. All the sinful acts in all of history. He was innocent and had never personally done any one of those things Himself, but He took on each and every one of them as if they were His own. What an act of love! What a gift!

No wonder He pleaded if it was possible to find another way! No wonder He sweat heavy drops! He became everything we are, and everything He was not.

The Bible explains that this was the plan that God--Father, Son and Holy Spirit--talked through and prepared for before the world was even created. Before sin had ever happened. The plan was queued up and ready, and when it was necessary, They put that plan into action.

In physical terms, Jesus experienced death by crucifixion. In spiritual terms, Jesus' death made us right with God.

Why didn't God just forgive all sinners rather than go through all that? Why didn't He just say to Adam and Eve, "Let's just do a reset here and start over as if this day in the garden never happened?"

The Bible clearly declares that God is love. He doesn't just demonstrate love. He IS love. Which means everything He does is motivated and guided by love. Because He is love, He is not able to just wink at or turn His eye away from sin and rebellion. To "just forgive and move on" is to not take sin seriously, nor does it address the root of the sin problem. One of God's core values is justice for all, and justice does not blindly pardon those who are guilty. His challenge is how to love and how to be just all at the same time.

Picture a home with a family of five children. One of the rules in this home is that lying will not be tolerated, in any way, and there will be appropriate consequences should it ever occur.

Now imagine that the oldest child makes up a lie about one of the other siblings. A totally fabricated lie. The child who the lie is made up about gets into trouble and suffers the consequences for an act that she did not even commit. The child knows that she was wrongly punished because she knows she didn't commit the act and is totally innocent.

In due time, the facts play themselves out. It becomes obvious that the oldest child did in fact make the tale up in the first place, and now the younger child has already suffered as a result. The one who lied, the one who was punished, and the other three siblings all have a vested interest in what the parents do now.

The parents have at least two options. One is to simply ignore what the oldest child did, pretend the whole event never happened, and just move on with life. Basically, they would be saying, "Let's just do a reset." If they choose that option what happens to the child who has already suffered the consequences of the lie? Her view of the parents would become troubled and tainted. Any anger that may arise would be understandable. Trust in her parents would be damaged.

The child who told the lie could come to believe that "Our parents don't really mean what they say. I could probably do this again and get away with it."

And the three who are watching from the sideline are now confused on what they can believe or trust about what the parents say.

On the other hand, should the parents follow through now that the truth is known, and the specified consequences are experienced by the child who lied, the younger child now rests in the fact that the parents are in fact acting with fairness and justice appropriate to the circumstances. Trust in the parents is restored as they have demonstrated that their word is in fact dependable.

The one who started the whole drama by lying in the first place realizes that the parents mean what they say and that they ultimately have the best interest of the whole family at heart.

And finally, the observing siblings are at peace, because they are first-hand witnesses to the fact that the parents will not make excuses or blur the lines that have been drawn up.

We have the same scenario here. God is the parent. Adam and Eve are guilty, and the devil and his angels, as well as the angels in Heaven are looking on, interested to observe how God will handle this.

In the situation before Him in Eden, God knew that justice must remain in place because justice is a core value of God's Universe. However, love and mercy must also remain in place because God IS love. He was not willing to just destroy sinners in an act of justice, nor was He able to just wink, pretending it didn't happen. Through His wisdom He was able to provide an option that would demonstrate His love and His justice.

Somewhere in a discussion in Heaven, the Father, Son and Holy Spirit considered how to respond to a dilemma such as this. It must have been acknowledged that "Justice doesn't allow us to set aside the consequences, but one option would be that we could suffer the consequences ourselves so that these we created don't have to." It was decided that it would be God the Son who would come to Earth as a man named Jesus to save His people from their sins.

When Jesus died, the sun was hidden and darkness crowded around the cross for a period of three hours. At that time, in utter anguish, Jesus cried out, "My God, My God, why have You abandoned me?" Sin and sinners cannot exist in the direct presence of a Holy God. Because Jesus was taking our sin upon Himself, God could not draw near to comfort His own Son.

A false scenario that has arisen from this, no doubt prompted by the enemy, suggests that this demonstrates that God is an angry, demanding God, not satisfied until someone dies for sin. The picture is painted that God is motivated by revenge, so, because Jesus loves us He came and died and then turned and sharply said to His Father, "There, is that good enough!? Are you happy now that someone has died?" I want to assure you that this is a false representation of what actually took place.

Instead, Jesus, by choice, willingly came to Earth to die in our place. He offered Himself as God in human flesh. He became human so He could die. He lived a perfect life, then died as a sinner. It was the ideal and appropriate way to exhibit God's love, and God's justice. He didn't excuse sinners. This demonstrates justice. But sinners did not have to suffer the consequences of sin. He took our sins upon Himself, proving how much we matter to Him. This demonstrates love.

This was the message that God wanted to instill into sinful humanity when He instructed them to sacrifice animals as an act of confession of their sins. It's horrific to think about, but so is the nature of sin to God. He wanted people to understand in graphic terms that death is the inevitable result of sin, yet because of an offered sacrifice dying in their place instead, they could escape death and be able to live.

The sacrificial system of the Sanctuary services was designed to display a picture of what the coming Savior of the world would experience on their behalf. The offerings and rituals they carried out painted a picture of what Jesus would ultimately endure instead of us.

When Abraham was asked to sacrifice his only, promised son, he set out to obey. At the last minute he was stopped by the voice of an angel and congratulated on his faith, proving that he would not hold back anything, even the son he had waited so long for. He was totally surrendered to God. It was then that Abraham noticed a ram caught in the bushes which became the sacrifice in Isaac's place. This provided another symbolic picture of Jesus who would die in our place and allow us to live forever.

When the Hebrew people had crossed the Red Sea, they were in need of water during their wilderness journey. Moses struck the rock as instructed and life-giving water gushed forth. Jesus is described in the Bible as the water of life, and He is also described as the solid rock.

At the end of the forty years, when Moses was asked by God to simply speak to the rock and in his anger at the people he struck it twice instead, God could not just wink at that. His Son Jesus was to be struck, or crucified, once, on the cross. He only needed to die once. From then on, He is to be spoken to in prayer as we come to seek His life-giving resources. He will never have to die again. God instructed Moses to simply speak to the rock that day. Instead, Moses struck the rock twice, after it had been struck once already forty years earlier. He was not obedient to the voice of God, and his action was a misrepresentation of the accurate picture of Jesus.

When Jesus said, "Whoever believes in me will not perish, but have eternal life," He offers Himself for us, and then lets us choose. We can let His death be for us, in our place, or we can live as we choose and then die (or perish) for ourselves.

When we believe that Jesus is the answer to our need for eternal life, and personally acknowledge that to Him, God does the most amazing thing! At that moment He DECLARES us to be righteous. In other words, we are "made right" with God. God does not lie or exaggerate. We were born with the sin gene already deeply implanted in our heart and mind, but when God declares us to be righteous because of our faith in the righteous Jesus, we are indeed righteous.

Jesus was righteous, sinless in every way, and yet died as the sinful me. Then He offers, "I'll trade you! If you believe in me, I'll declare you to be righteous, just like I was!"

That's why Jesus qualifies. That's why ALL nations on Earth are blessed because of Him. No matter of race, gender, or creed, every single person on Earth once again has a choice. God never forces, He simply offers, invites, and hopes we will choose Him, but He ultimately leaves the choice up to us. When we profess our belief in Him, we are in that moment born again with a spiritual heart. In that act, God declares us to be His. What a gracious God!

Grace simply means that we get what we don't deserve. That is God's offer, through Jesus.

I invite you to bring to mind a person you may know who suffers deep pain from their past choices. Regrets, failures, and dark memories flood their minds. Guilt is their constant companion and hangs around like a dense cloud. Maybe that describes you. What teacher, belief or philosophy has the power to provide forgiveness and peace to that person? I can tell you with assurance, there is no book, catch-phrase, teaching, or mantra able to accomplish that. There is no person, pastor, priest, or pope that can offer such a gift. Only Jesus! The God who became man, lived a perfect life and offered it to sinners, provides the only solution. His sacrificial blood offers a cleansing of the heart and a peace that passes understanding that can be found nowhere else. To search for that solution in any other place only brings futility and disappointment.

What if it's true?

BIBLE TEXTS THAT DECLARE THIS THEME:

- "Purify me from my sins, and I will be clean; wash me and I will be whiter than snow." Psalm 51:7

188

- "This High Priest of ours (Jesus) understands our weaknesses, for he faced all of the same testing we do, yet he did not sin." Hebrews 4:15

- "But he was pierced for our rebellion, crushed for our sins. He was beaten so we could be whole. He was whipped so we could be healed. All of us, like sheep, have strayed away. We have left God's paths to follow our own. Yet the Lord laid on him the sins of us all." Isaiah 53:5, 6

- "For He made Him who knew no sin to be sin for us, that we might become the righteousness of God in Him." 2 Corinthians 5:21 (NKJV)

- "But God showed his great love for us by sending Christ to die for us while we were still sinners." Roman 5:8

- "For you know that God paid a ransom to save you from the empty life you inherited from your ancestors. It was not paid with mere gold or silver, which lose their value. It was the precious blood of Christ, the sinless, spotless Lamb of God. God chose him as your ransom long before the world began, but now in these last days he has been revealed for your sake." 1 Peter 1:18-20

- "He (Christ) loved us and offered himself as a sacrifice for us." Ephesians 5:2

- "For God's will was for us to be made holy by the sacrifice of the body of Jesus Christ once for all time." Hebrews 10:10

- "Christ suffered for our sins once for all time. He never sinned, but he died for sinners to bring you safely home to God."1 Peter 3:18

- "I passed on to you what was most important and what had also been passed on to me. Christ died for our sins, just as the Scriptures said." 1 Corinthians 15:3

- "Yet God, in his grace, freely makes us right in his sight. He did this through Christ Jesus when he freed us from the penalty for our sins." Romans 3:24

- "For God presented Jesus as the sacrifice for sin. People are made right with God when they believe that Jesus sacrificed his life, shedding his blood. This shows that God was being fair when he held back and did not punish those who sinned in times past." Romans 3:25

- "God did this to demonstrate his righteousness, for he himself is fair and just, and he declares sinners to be right in his sight when they believe in Jesus." Romans 3:26

- "For even the Son of Man came not to be served but to serve others and to give his life as a ransom for many." Matthew 20:28

- "God is Love." 1 John 4:8

- "For this is how God loved the world: He gave his one and only son, so that everyone who believes in him will not perish but have eternal life." John 3:16

- "And now that you belong to Christ, you are the true children of Abraham. You are his heirs, and God's promise to Abraham belongs to you." Galatians 3:29

18

JESUS ANSWERS LIFE'S
FOUR MAJOR QUESTIONS

Where did I come from and how did I get here?

The Bible informs us that "God created everything through him [Jesus], and nothing was created except through him." John 1:3. We came from the hand of a loving Creator. It was Jesus Himself. We are not here by chance, or by some perplexing theory involving millions of years. We are here by design. Created with intricate detail, we have the privilege to exist, love, and live in relationship with God and others.

Is there a purpose and meaning for my life?

Those who design and create things do not do their work without a goal in mind. Contractors do not nail boards together without reason. Seamstresses do not sew pieces of cloth together just for something to do. There is always a plan. The purpose Jesus had in mind when He created us was for relationship and to demonstrate His character by being created in His image. He wanted us to experience the love He planned to share with us, and He wanted us to enjoy the experience of loving Him and others. Everything Jesus did by coming to Earth to comfort us and save us from our sins was motivated totally by the loving heart of God to restore us to that original purpose which was lost in Eden.

How do we explain the relationship between the good and evil we see in the world?

Many wonder how there can be a powerful and loving God and yet evil, violence and death remain in His presence? If God is powerful and loving, why does this not end? The answer comes to light in the events surrounding the crucifixion of Jesus. The enemy of God demonstrated a depth of anger and hatred unknown anywhere else or at any time in history. The fact that he could motivate people to the extent of crucifying the Son of God exposed the true motive behind anything that he did or continues to do. On the flip side, the fact that the Son of God would allow Himself to be crucified when He was powerful enough to destroy all His enemies with a blink of an eye revealed the depth of the love of God. At the cross, both motives are demonstrated in such vivid clarity that we are left with the assurance that God will, in His time, eradicate the work of the enemy once and for all.

What happens when I die? Is this all there is?

Because God has allowed the wages of sin to play out within our very existence, we understand the full impact of our condition. However, even though we now face death, which is a dreadful reality we have no control over, God chose to step in to give us an option. So, no this is not all there is, unless we choose to let it be. Through Jesus Christ's death and resurrection, life and death as we know it on planet Earth is NOT all there is. Through Jesus we are able to move beyond death to eternal life in the peaceful, loving atmosphere God had designed for us way back in the beginning.

19

THE REST OF THE STORY

All stories have an ending. The Bible does too, but the events that bring an end to the Bible story, as well as an end to all things on planet Earth as we know them, are yet to happen in the future. We are still here; we are not in Heaven yet. The Bible has revealed to us what God's ultimate plan for us is and to remind us that we are not experiencing anywhere near what He had hoped for all the nations of the Earth.

We have followed the theme through the Bible on how sin entered our world, and how God has demonstrated that He will stop at nothing in order to bring us back into a meaningful relationship with Him.

We have been introduced to Jesus Christ, the Messiah, (which means promised deliverer) who came in human flesh, and who alone qualifies as the One to be able to redeem and restore us.

And here we are, still locked into a world that offers continued and deepening chaos and troubles. Overall life is not improving. We are forced to deal with new sickness and diseases. Families still break up. Political tension is increasing with no sign of relief. And, we still make too many trips to graveyards, well aware that one day it will be our turn to stay behind as our friends say good-bye to us and go home.

If Jesus came to fix it all, why isn't it fixed? Why isn't it over? The good news is that the Bible promises and predicts an amazing and exciting wrap-up to it all.

One time I was speaking with a man I had just met about his perspective on life and the future of the world. I shared with him a quick snapshot of my Biblical worldview and what I understand the future to look like. He sadly said, "I wish I could believe that Bill, but I don't think so. I believe that one day the Earth is going to move a little closer to the sun and we are all going to burn to a crisp, or it's going to move a little further away from the sun and we are all going to freeze to death. We won't know it's coming until it happens, and it will be over just like that. No future, no Heaven, no eternity. It's depressing I know, but that's how I see it."

Thankfully, the Bible spells out a very different conclusion than his, one which leaves us with anticipation, courage, and hope.

It is now almost two thousand years since Jesus promised He would come back to get us. In fact, in the book of Revelation it quotes Him to say, "Behold I come quickly." Two thousand years seems a little excessive and as a result many have doubted that He will ever come again. We think in terms of minutes and seconds, microwave cooking and fast-food drive-up windows. We are a hurry-up people, and twenty centuries does not jive with the word "quickly."

When the apostle Peter wrote his letters, he reminded us that a thousand years of our time is like a day to God. We do not have the same concept of time that God does so all we can do is trust that the promised events will take place regardless of how long it takes to experience them.

Peter explains that a delay on God's part for Jesus' return is actually a good thing for us in that He is giving more time for people to meet Him, know Him, and choose to believe in Him. He added that God is patient because He does not want anyone to lose out.

When Jesus ascended to Heaven right before the disciples' very eyes, the angels standing by assured them that Jesus would in fact come again in the very same way that they saw Him leave. What they meant was that He would come physically, just as He was when He left, and instead of ascending, He would descend this time. They assured the disciples, and us, that we would all see Him again.

In fact, we are told that in some miraculous manner, God will make it happen that "every eye" will see Him when He comes again. I'm not sure how that will happen on this round ball we call Earth, but God said it, so I have to leave it to Him to take care of the details. It's going to be dazzling and incredible. Unlike any event ever in human history.

It is estimated that there are approximately eighteen hundred and forty-five Biblical references to the second coming of Jesus. His first coming in Bethlehem provided the guarantee of restoration. His second coming will turn the promise of restoration into reality.

There are several signs and indicators that have been prophesied as to what we will see and experience just before He comes back. Like road signs giving us a progress report of miles traveled and how close we are to our destination, these unfolding events give us reason to believe there is not much time left until we see Jesus again. Bible students and scholars are generally in agreement and confident that we are on the verge of having it all come true.

Here's what we can look forward to. Imagine this!

It's going to be anything but a secret arrival. Jesus said that when He comes it will be as brilliant as if lightning were to shine all the way from the east to the west.

It's also going to be noisy! He will come from Heaven to Earth on a bank of clouds, surrounded by angels. Thousands upon thousands of them. There will be a trumpet sound that we will all hear, and there will be a shout from His voice to let us know He's back, just like He promised.

That trumpet sound, along with the call of His voice, will be miraculous enough that everyone who has died believing in Him will awaken from their graves. This is the exact moment that the enemy we call death is finally defeated forever. The resurrection of Jesus was the guarantee that His children who die would rise again also. When the resurrection of God's people everywhere takes place, it will be the fulfillment and realization of that guarantee.

195

I remember being at the funeral of a man in his forties where his mother stood to speak to the family and friends who had gathered. She said, "I spoke to him, and I tried to wake him up! But I couldn't." Then she confidently and emphatically added, "But I know Someone who can!" She was referring to Jesus and what He will do when He comes back. Her faith and confidence that Jesus would be able to bring her son back to life at that time was inspiring to us all.

My wife and I have personally experienced the loss of a daughter to cancer. She was also a sister and an auntie. We all miss her! There is an empty hole in our hearts. But we live in peace, courage and in the hope that we will see her alive and vibrant again on the day Jesus returns. That helps to take the sting out of it all.

There will be some who are still alive when He comes back, looking for and expecting His return. Those who have died and are then resurrected by the calling voice of Jesus will come from their graves and join with those who are still alive. Together, they will all be lifted off the Earth at the same time to join Jesus and His host of angels for the trip back to Heaven.

The day that Jesus returns is the exact time that humanity will receive the restored gift of immortality. We are told that we will be changed in a moment, "in the twinkling of an eye," and from that day on we will never experience death in any form ever again.

But there is still a missing piece. What happens to those who did not believe in Jesus when they died?

Jesus explained that there will be two resurrections. This is significant information, especially since it is coming from the very One who will be doing the resurrecting. His statement is both comforting and sobering.

The first resurrection is the one we have just talked about, for those who died believing a Savior would come again and resurrect them so they too could enjoy Heaven and eternal life. Those who lived and died back in the Old Testament didn't know Jesus by name or person, but demonstrated their belief in a savior as they brought their sacrificial offerings to the Sanctuary service. We who now know about the details of Jesus' sacrifice can express our belief in Him personally through prayer. This is why that veil in the temple was torn in two when Jesus died. Animal sacrifices were no longer necessary.

I have a close relative whose infant daughter died a crib death at the age of three months old. It appeared to me that this mother had no measurable interest in God from that time on. I was talking to her many decades after that, and we talked about God. She became resistant, even angry, then blurted out, "Where was God when my baby died?"

Such a fair and relevant question. I suddenly realized the reason for the depth of her resistance to God. We talked about her question, and I shared my understanding of the work of God's enemy in our lives. I assured her that death is always the work of the devil and that it was not her fault that her baby died, (even though her husband had told her it was). Nor was it the work of an angry God that took her baby's life.

I do not know her heart after that conversation. I don't know if she resolved things with Him before she passed away. But I trust her heart into God's hands, and I am confident He will do what is right for her.

For those who die believing in Jesus, death is merely a sleep experience, from which Jesus will wake His people up when He comes to give them their reward. Those who have chosen not to accept God's Son, and who are not looking forward to His coming will die at the time of His return simply because they are not able to be in the presence of a Holy God whom they have chosen to reject.

Many people believe in Heaven and talk about it as commonplace, although I am not aware of anyone who has been there to be able to tell us what it's like. The Bible describes it as a place with streets paved of gold and mansions to live in. We are told that Heaven has a capital city called New Jerusalem, the description of which challenges the imagination. One of the greatest assets is that we will once again have access to the Tree of Life that Adam and Eve were not able to eat from anymore after they chose to put their trust in the enemy.

After Jesus returns and takes those who have trusted in Him to Heaven, for a period of the first one thousand years we will settle into the beauty and reality of a restored relationship with God. In Heaven, far away from all the darkness we once lived in. This will be a time when we clarify any questions we had with God, or about God, and He will answer us in ways that leave us completely at peace. For example, this is a time when my family and I will get to hear the events around our daughter's sickness and death through God's eyes, and He will tell us things we would have had no way of knowing. And, the best part is, that she will be there to hear it too!

The Bible then explains that after those thousand years are over there will be another resurrection. This one is much more sobering. Jesus calls the first one at the time of His second coming the resurrection of life, and He calls this second one the resurrection of judgment. This is the resurrection of those who died, either before or at the time of His coming, choosing not to accept or follow the Creator God or believe in Jesus who came to die for them.

God loves and respects everyone the same. He cannot not love. His essence IS love. As hard as it is to comprehend, the fact is that some choose to not love Him. The enemy of God was once the highest-ranking angel in Heaven, living in the very presence of God, and yet even there chose to turn his back on Him. He was also able to convince one third of the angels in Heaven to rebel against God along with him. God never forces anyone to love him, so He allowed them all to exercise their free will. He let them turn away from Him if they wanted to even though He knew it was to their own detriment.

That is what a God of love does. He invites, and then because He loves, He honors the decisions each one makes. While His choice would be to have every person on Earth join Him and benefit from His restoration plan, it just is not going to be so.

God is the judge of the universe. He will weigh the circumstances and the influences that have caused people to choose Him or not choose Him. He is holy and will make fair and honest judgment regarding each individual. He sees things that we can never see in the hearts and lives of people, and His final judgment regarding everyone will be absolutely just and fair. Jesus assured us in His conversation with Nicodemus that "God did not send His Son into the world to condemn the world, but that the world through Him might be saved." John 3:17

Those who have died having no interest in God, or what He had to offer through Jesus, will come to life again at this second resurrection. At this time, when they come to life and see Jesus and the angels in person, they will acknowledge that there truly is a God, and Jesus is His Son, as He claimed. They will recall opportunities they had been given to accept God into their lives but had chosen to make other decisions instead.

This is the one and only time in history that all people who have ever lived on the planet will be alive at the same time. The Bible says that every knee will bow, and every tongue will confess that Jesus is Lord. Some will do it through praise and worship, while others will simply acknowledge it because the evidence is so clear it cannot be denied. There will be only these two groups of people.

It is at this time that each one will be granted the choice they have made. For those who have made the choice to be with Him, their wish was already granted when Jesus took them to Heaven a thousand years earlier, at the time of the first resurrection. For those who have made the decision not to be with Him, God now sadly grants them their wish. These will die a permanent death. It's not revenge; it's simply His work of honoring each individual's choice. This death is referred to in the Bible as the second death. When God said to Adam and Eve, "You will surely die," this is the death He was speaking about. The coming of Jesus to our planet is what provided another option. Thank you Jesus!

When all of these events are completed, it is at this time we are told that God Himself will wipe every tear from our eyes and there will be no more death or sorrow or crying or pain. It's impossible to imagine it when we are surrounded by so much crying, pain and loss right now.

The last crowning touch of the story is that God will bring Heaven, His throne, His presence and all of us who dwell there with Him back down to this Earth and we will all take up residence here again. With Him! He will recreate it all anew, beautiful and perfect, the way it was when He first created it. The final act of restoration is now complete, only better because God will inhabit planet Earth, right here along with us.

No matter how wonderful we might imagine Heaven and eternity to be, we aren't even close. We are told that our eyes have not seen, nor have our ears heard, the things that God has in store for us. So, we will get to discover, explore and inspect the whole universe, and find out for ourselves. And the new reality will never end!

BIBLE TEXTS THAT DECLARE THIS THEME:

- Jesus to His disciples, "Don't let your hearts be troubled. Trust in God, and trust also in me. There is more than enough room in my Father's home. If this were not so, would I have told you that I am going to prepare a place for you? When everything is ready, I will come and get you, so that you will always be with me where I am." John 14:1-3

- Angels to the disciples, "Men of Galilee, why are you standing here staring into heaven? Jesus has been taken from you into heaven, but someday he will return from heaven in the same way you saw him go!" Acts 1:11

- "Look! He comes with the clouds of heaven. And every eye will see him." Revelation 1:7 NASB

- "For as the lightning flashes in the east and shines to the west, so it will be when the Son of Man comes." Matthew 24:27

- "Just as everyone dies because we all belong to Adam, everyone who belongs to Christ will be given new life. But there is an order to this resurrection: Christ was raised as the first of the harvest; then all who belong to Christ will be raised when he comes back." 1 Corinthians 15:22,23

- Paul speaking, "But let me reveal to you a wonderful secret. We will not all die, but we will all be transformed. It will happen in a moment, in the blink of an eye, when the last trumpet is blown. For when the trumpet sounds, those who have died will be raised to live forever. And we who are living will also be transformed. For our dying bodies must be transformed into bodies that will never die; our mortal bodies must be transformed into immortal bodies. . . . For sin is the sting that results in death, . . . but thank God! He gives us victory over sin and death through our Lord Jesus Christ." 1 Corinthians 15:51-57

- Paul speaking, "For the Lord himself will come down from heaven with a commanding shout, with the voice of the archangel, and with the trumpet call of God. First the believers who have died will rise from their graves. Then, together with them, we who are still alive and remain on the earth will be caught up in the clouds to meet the Lord in the air. Then we will be with the Lord forever." 1 Thessalonians 4:16,17.

- Paul speaking, "As for me, my life has already been poured out as an offering to God. The time of my death is near. I have fought the good fight. I have finished the race, and I have remained faithful. And now the prize awaits me—the crown of righteousness, which the Lord, the righteous Judge, will give me on the day of his return. And the prize is not just for me but for all who eagerly look forward to his appearing." 1 Timothy 4:6-8

- Jesus speaking, "Indeed, the time is coming when all the dead in their graves will hear the voice of God's Son, and they will rise again. Those who have done good will rise to experience eternal life, and those who have continued in evil will rise to experience judgment." John 5: 28, 29

- But you must not forget this one thing, dear friends: A day is like a thousand years to the Lord, and a thousand years is like a day. The Lord isn't really being slow about his promise, as some people think. No, he is being patient for your sake. He does not want anyone to be destroyed, but wants everyone to repent. 2 Peter 3:8,9

- Referring to those who died trusting in God and Jesus: "They all came to life again, and they reigned with Christ for a thousand years. This is the first resurrection. (The rest of the dead did not come back to life until the thousand years had ended.) Blessed and holy are those who share in the first resurrection. For them the second death holds no power." Revelation 20:4-6

- "And I saw the holy city, the new Jerusalem, coming down from God out of heaven like a bride beautifully dressed for her husband. I heard a loud shout from the throne, saying, 'Look, God's home is now among his people! He will live with them, and they will be his people. God himself will be with them. He will wipe every tear from their eyes, and there will be no more death or sorrow or crying or pain. All these things are gone forever." Revelation 21:2-4

- "No eye has seen, no ear has heard, and no mind has imagined what God has prepared for those who love him." 1 Corinthians 2:9

A WORD ABOUT HELL

It is important that I say something about hell and hell fire.

The Bible clearly states there will be a fire to cleanse the earth after those thousand years are finished. At Noah's flood, those who did not go into the ark perished in the waters that covered the earth. Jesus has offered Himself as the ark of safety for anyone who wants to live forever with Him, but He has also warned that those who choose not to accept His gift will perish. Jesus never refers to perish as a tortuous eternal life of burning in anguish. Perish means a final separation, the full meaning of death. Death that is not just a time of sleep.

This cleansing work will be done with fire and when its work is complete, the fire will go out. All fires go out when there is no fuel left to burn. The Bible does refer to the smoke of the fires of hell going up forever and ever, which is simply a Bible metaphor to say that nothing will put that fire out. It will not be extinguished by any outside source, but when its work is done it will go out on its own.

In the Bible we read about the cities of Sodom and Gomorrah which were destroyed by supernatural fire during the time of Abraham. Jude 1:7 says, "And don't forget Sodom and Gomorrah and their neighboring towns, . . .Those cities were destroyed by fire and serve as a warning of the eternal fire of God's judgment."

The judgment was eternal. Those cities near the Dead Sea have never been rebuilt, but the "eternal fire of God's judgment" on those cities is not still burning today. God makes it clear that He will cleanse the earth of all sin, but His loving heart is not in any way interested in torturing people, let alone forever and ever.

Malachi, in the Old Testament, tells us that sin and sinners will be like "dust under our feet." Malachi 4:6 Obviously they are not burning forever.

Whichever choice we make will be forever in its result. We will either be separated from God forever, or we will live with Him forever.

This is only a very light touch on a big topic that entire books have been devoted to, but it is necessary to at least address it.

WHAT IF IT'S TRUE?

C. S. LEWIS SAYS

I am trying here to prevent anyone saying the really foolish thing that people often say about Him: I'm ready to accept Jesus as a great moral teacher, but I don't accept his claim to be God. That is the one thing we must not say. A man who is merely a man and said the sort of things Jesus said would not be a great moral teacher. He would either be a lunatic, -- on the level with a man who says he is a poached egg – or else he would be the Devil of Hell. You must make your choice. Either this man was, and is, the Son of God, or else a madman or something worse. You can shut him up for a fool, you can spit at him and kill him as a demon or you can fall at his feet and call him Lord and God, but let us not come up with any patronizing nonsense about his being a great human teacher. He has not left that open to us. He did not intend to.

C.S LEWIS, MERE CHRISTIANITY

* * * * *

Genesis 1–The world is created in perfection
Genesis 2–God's created children live in His presence, in paradise
Genesis 3–Sin is introduced

Revelation 20–Sin is destroyed once and for all
Revelation 21–God again takes up residence with His children
Revelation 22–All things are re-created anew, paradise restored!

God is the ultimate victor and His children reap the benefits!

20

IF IT'S TRUE

So, there you have it, the Bible in a few pages. What will you do with the story and the eternal themes that are embedded within it?

Of course, a decision needs to be made about whether the Bible can be trusted. It was not my intent to prove the Bible to be true. There are many books that do a much better job than I could on that topic.

Should one decide the Bible is not trustworthy, for whatever reason or reasons, then the Bible is just a tale, and they can simply move on into reading the next book of interest. The worst thing that happened by reading this book is that it cost a few hours of time.

I think back to Abraham Lincoln's question. "Saying a dog's tail is a leg, does not make it a leg." If it is proven beyond a doubt that the Bible is not valid or trustworthy, that is one thing. However, simply stating "I just do not believe the Bible to be true," setting it aside and moving on, is a risky move. The declarations of the Bible carry enormous consequences.

If, on the other hand, one believes the Bible to be trustworthy, valid and true, then there are really only two options. The reader must decide what to do with the eternal and universal truth that is presented there.

Josh McDowell summed it up this way. He has a great chart outlining his thoughts which is summarized like this: Either Jesus was right when He claimed to be the Son of God, or He was wrong. If He was wrong, there would be two options. He would be either delusional, or a liar. In fact, McDowell says, if He was wrong, He must have been a lunatic because He died for His belief.

However, if He was right, then there are also only two options. One can believe His words and receive all that He has to offer, or one can reject His words, and experience the consequences of that decision. (The New Evidence That Demands a Verdict, pg. 158. 1999 Thomas Nelson Publishers)

If it's true, here is what we must consider.

We were created by the marvelous action of a loving and powerful Creator God.

Because the first parents disobeyed and turned their back on God, they experienced the consequence of death and passed that mortal condition on to all descendants born after them.

We are, without any input on the matter, born into a condition of living a life less than what God wants for us, including facing death as the inevitable conclusion.

None of us do life right all the time, and our human condition completely explains why. We are all on the same downward trajectory. We demonstrate the human condition on a regular basis by the way we talk, act and respond to the challenges of life, sometimes in hurtful, even destructive ways.

Like any loving parent, God is not willing to let us go without doing everything He can to win us back.

God is not able to shrug and simply step over the wages of sin. He cannot just ignore our condition and forgive us, pretending it never happened. Sin is already embedded within us. Merely forgiving us for our actions without dealing with the sin issue of the heart would be like putting a Band-Aid on a gaping wound.

Like gravity that never stops pulling, sin has an unrelenting and ultimate outcome, which is death. Death is total separation from God, from His restoration plan, and from eternal life. Forever.

God chose to insert Himself into the gap for us and do for us what we could not do for ourselves. In order to accomplish this for us, He had to be born as a human being, just like us.

Jesus, (AKA as God the Son), came to dwell with us, as one of us, in our broken condition. He lived a perfect, sinless life, never once wavering or giving in to the enemy as Adam and Eve had done. He lived a life totally unworthy of death, but was crucified and died on our behalf, because He took on the guilt of our individual sins as if He was us.

In doing so, and then being resurrected again, He defeated death so that death is no longer the only option for us. Because of Him we now have a choice, once again, as to whether we want to die forever or to live forever.

We can choose to do nothing with Jesus or any of what the Bible teaches about Him and continue to live our lives the way we want to live them. The reward will be the total amount of enjoyment we are able to pack into the few years we have to live before we die.

OR,

We can choose to believe in Him, be born again, which is to trade our broken lives for His perfect one. By doing that we will enjoy all the benefits He has to offer in this life as well as enjoy the total restoration plan He has put in place for all who accept His free gift.

We can't earn it, but we can humbly open our hearts and receive it.

It is a free gift that we cannot earn in any way. But it does cost us. We give up our "right" to make choices that please our minds and bodies like Eve did. Instead of decisions that serve only our pleasures and self-centered goals, we will experience the perks that God gives by choosing to be an apprentice of Jesus, learning to seek His input and guidance in life.

He invited people to "Follow Me." Being an apprentice means that if we accept the invitation to follow, we will learn to love the way He loved, and we will enjoy the reward of giving. We will learn the satisfaction of looking at others the way He did, realizing that everyone has a story in their background, and needs to be loved for who they are. We will have a reason for a hope and a future that will last forever, in the presence and community of people who want to live by those same values as well. And we will once again enjoy the relationship with Him that God envisioned for us at the time of creation.

The question is for all of us. It is for you, the reader, personally.

What If It's True?

If it is, what will you do with Jesus?

You now have the opportunity to choose. Maybe some things will change for you, but ultimately all for the better. Jesus said, "You are truly my disciples if you remain faithful to my teachings. You will know the truth, and the truth will set you free." John 8:32.

Free from what?

Free from the guilt and penalty of the sinful nature.

Free from the fear of death.

Free from the hopelessness of life if viewed only from a horizontal perspective.

Free from past regrets and failures.

Free from the questions about "what comes after this?"

Free from the fear that I'm not doing enough for God.

Free from the power of God's enemy in my life.

Free to enjoy all the good things God has planned.

Some are afraid of how much their life will change in order to follow God. There is no question that the human heart's search for all things pleasurable and selfish will adjust. Aspects of the journey are hard because by following God we declare war on His enemy who wants to destroy God's children or at least make their lives miserable.

It's hard to go upstream against the human condition. The human heart does not like the word "submission." It's also hard to just give in and go with the flow because it will ultimately end in eternal destruction.

So, we get to choose our "hard". The choice we make also chooses the consequence of that choice.

EPILOGUE

This book is a quick peak inside my spiritual heart. I love what God has taught us in the Bible. I love the Jesus who is revealed there. I am one who has fallen short of God's desire for my life, and the Bible tells me I should not be surprised by that, for ALL have fallen short. I do not worry about it though because of Jesus. He came to hang out with people like me, and He would welcome me to the dinner table where He was invited to eat with the tax collectors and sinners. I qualify to have a place at His table.

And so do you. You matter to Him every bit as much as I do.

That's why I wrote the book. I just wanted to tell you about Jesus. I included the whole story so you could see Him in the full setting of history, making it clear why He shines so bright. We who live here on this planet are SO in need of Him.

I have attempted to make it as simple as possible and yet I always wonder if I have said it "right."

It is my deep prayer that as you have read these pages you have seen that Jesus is not just a swear word, He is a Holy Friend. He is God, and yet He is gentle with broken and bruised people. He is majestic and He also loves to pause and listen to all who are drawn to Him. He is the only one who can give us that which our hearts need more than anything else.

I am blessed to know that you have taken the time to stay with me this long. I have one goal and that is that the time and words I have invested will make an eternal difference in your life. Maybe we will have a chance to talk about it someday.

If you want to connect and chat about what you have read here, you are welcome to reach out to me at:
bjspangler@shaw.ca or
403-302-0562

ACKNOWLEDGEMENTS

My first and deepest gratitude is to God, whose story is the reason I have for living with hope and anticipation for the future that is yet to come. His Son, Jesus, and the Holy Spirit who makes Jesus real to us, provide the passion and motivation for me to put these words on paper.

I am grateful for people who took time to give feedback, make suggestions and assist me in giving it my best.

My wife, Gwen, continually encouraged me to put in whatever time it took even though it meant that she was alone many hours while I sat before my keyboard and screen. She understood the passion I had for this book and supported me at every step to get it completed. She also read the manuscript carefully, catching typos and offering invaluable suggestions.

I want to say thanks to Stephen Densmore and his photography skills that provided the cover image.

My daughter, Karin Ross, designed the cover and guided me on the design of the pages. Her graphic design skills always put the perfect finishing touch on any project she takes on. I appreciate her dedication to this task to help make the book represent the power of this topic.

I do not have enough words to express my appreciation for my editor, Heather Russell. This is the second book she has worked on with me. She scrutinized every page, multiple times. Reading, suggesting, correcting, then reading again. Her attention to grammatical detail provides a much more readable book for you. However, as appreciative as I am for her editing skills, I also acknowledge that this book is better than it would have been had I done it alone without the input, guidance, and suggestions she shared with me along the way. Her insights and creativity on how to manage and organize words help make these pages come alive.

RELATED BOOKS YOU MAY ENJOY

Here is a short list of a few books that are meaningful to me on a few of these topics that may be helpful to you should you choose to dig deeper into some of the ideas I have shared in these pages.

The New Evidence That Demands a Verdict, by Josh McDowell, Copyright 1999. Printed by Thomas Nelson Publishers

Forensic Faith, by J. Warner Wallace, Copyright 2017, Published by David C. Cook

Cold Case Christianity, by J. Warner Wallace, Copyright 2013, Published by David C. Cook

The Case for Christ, by Lee Strobel, Published by Zondervan

You Can Trust the Bible, by John R. W. Stott, Copyright 1991, Published by Discovery House Publishers

Sin and Salvation, by George R. Knight, Copyright 2008, Published by the Review and Herald Publishing Association

www.ingramcontent.com/pod-product-compliance
Lightning Source LLC
LaVergne TN
LVHW051256080426

835509LV00020B/3010